LEGENDS OF ANCIENT EGYPT

STORIES OF EGYPTIAN GODS AND HEROES

BY
F. H. BROOKSBANK B.A.

ILLUSTRATED BY
EVELYN PAUL

Copyright © 2018 Read Books Ltd.
This book is copyright and may not be
reproduced or copied in any way without
the express permission of the publisher in writing

British Library Cataloguing-in-Publication Data
A catalogue record for this book is available from
the British Library

LEGENDS OF ANCIENT EGYPT

The Death of Anthony

Foreword

EGYPT! What wondrous pictures are conjured up by that magic word! Scenes of white-robed priests moving in solemn procession through columned aisles to the sound of stately music; of shining warriors massed in dense array upon the burning plain, or charging irresistibly into the foeman's ranks; of royal pageants wherein King and Queen, bedecked in silks and cloth of gold, embroidered with a mine of gems, pass through the crowded lines of their acclaiming subjects; scenes of light and life and colour, which cannot fail to rouse our admiration, even our awe: such are some of the pictures that rise before us at the sound of the mystic name.

But ever do our thoughts come back to one supreme topic—the colossal structures always associated with our ideas of Egypt. Be it pyramid or temple, obelisk or sphinx that is painted in our dream, we are impressed with a sense of mystery, a wondering awe of the race that raised them. Who were these people, we ask ourselves, and what meant these mighty buildings wrought in enduring stone? What was the faith that inspired them to erect such marvellous temples to their gods? Something of the secret has been revealed to us within the last century, but much yet remains to be told.

Associated with the early faiths of all peoples are various legends that help us to understand how they grew and developed, how they came out of darkness into light. The story of the origin of our own race is rich in such traditions, and the myths of Greece and Rome are common knowledge. But in Egyptian story there is little to tell of the childhood stage of a people's development. Far as we can go back in their records, we always find Egypt in an advanced stage of civilization, with a religion removed almost entirely beyond the stage of myth. The one great legend connected with their faith is the story of the sufferings of Isis and her search for Osiris, her spouse, and even this is probably allegory rather than myth.

The faith professed by the Egyptians was as noble and sublime as any that the world has known. That it fell later into a confused belief in countless petty gods was due to priestcraft rather than to any fault in the faith itself. In all about them the Egyptians saw the hand of God—in the rising of the Nile and the fertilizing soil; in bird and beast, in sun and moon, in sky and earth and sea. But no mere nature-worshippers were they. The different aspects of nature which attracted their curiosity or commanded their awe were but symbols of a Supreme God, who manifested himself in all his works, and who must needs

Foreword

be honoured by the gift of the best of their handiwork.

So this people grew and rose to power, and in due time gave way to others. But their works could never die. The faith that inspired their daily life had given birth to monuments that truly seem everlasting. And there they remain, a silent witness to a people's greatness, when Egypt's glory has long since passed away.

F. H. B.

Contents

CHAPTER	PAGE
I. THE PEOPLE OF ANCIENT EGYPT	13
II. THE BELIEFS OF THE EGYPTIANS	20
III. THE BEGINNING OF ALL THINGS	30
IV. THE LIFE BEYOND	33
V. THE STORY OF RA AND ISIS	41

THE STORY OF ISIS AND OSIRIS

VI. THE KINGDOM OF OSIRIS	49
VII. THE QUEST OF ISIS	77
VIII. THE PERSECUTION BY TYPHON	104
IX. THE WORK OF HORUS	136

ANCIENT RULERS OF EGYPT

X. THE BUILDERS OF THE PYRAMIDS	151
XI. THE RIDDLE OF THE SPHINX	167
XII. THE GUARDIANS OF THE DESERT	172
XIII. THE BUILDERS OF THE TEMPLES	175
XIV. THE LADY OF THE OBELISKS	183
XV. THE JOURNEY OF KHENSU TO BEKHTEN	190
XVI. IN THE DAYS OF THE FAMINE	199

10 Egyptian Gods and Heroes

CHAPTER	PAGE
XVII. THE TREASURE-CHAMBER OF RHAMPSINITUS	204
XVIII. THE REIGN OF THE TWELVE KINGS	215
XIX. THE SHADOW OF THE END	222
XX. THE GLORY OF THE SUNSET	233
XXI. LIGHT UPON THE DARKNESS	252

Additional Egyptian Legends

I. THE COMING OF THE GREAT QUEEN	257

Illustrations

	PAGE
THE DEATH OF ANTHONY	*Frontispiece*
THE GOD THOTH	24
THE COMING OF OSIRIS AND ISIS	52
HORUS IN BATTLE	144
HAULING BLOCKS OF STONE FOR THE PYRAMIDS	156
RAMESES II DEFEATING THE KHETANS	180
THE TREASURE-CHAMBER OF RHAMPSINITUS	206

*Our birth is but a sleep and a forgetting;
The Soul that rises with us, our life's Star,
 Hath had elsewhere its setting
  And cometh from afar;
 Not in entire forgetfulness,
 And not in utter nakedness,
But trailing clouds of glory do we come
  From God, who is our home.*
      WM. WORDSWORTH

CHAPTER I

The People of Ancient Egypt

A LONG narrow strip of rich black soil, flanked on either side by seemingly endless wastes of sand, and running through its midst a broad grey stream, that opens at its mouth into a wide delta, such is Egypt. In the days of which our story tells, the delta was cut across by many narrow streams, that opened out here and there into wide morasses fringed with reeds and grass, and was in no wise the smiling land it is to-day.

The chief part of the country, then, was the long strip above the delta, and here the people mostly lived. They worked hard, early and late, depending for their living on the fruits of their toil in the black earth with which the river was so bountiful. But they were a warlike race, too, and in course of time their conquests extended far and wide, so that no other people could compare with them in wealth and power and dominion. In this they were helped by the great learning of their wise men, their ability, their enlightenment, above all, by their faith, by all that we to-day call civilization; for the Egyptians of six thousand years ago

14   Egyptian Gods and Heroes

were a race versed in earthly wisdom and heavenly lore.

The people were divided into classes, according to their work and position in the state, and no man might move from his class to another except with the consent of the King. But the poor people were not kept in a state of servility merely because they were poor. Many a man rose from a humble beginning to the highest offices in the land.

At the head of the nation stood the King. He was supreme in law, in war, and in religion. Nothing could be done without his consent. His will was the law, and no man would think of questioning his behests. He was the representative of God, nay, he traced his lineage to the Sun-God himself, and one of the names borne by every Egyptian king was Son of the Sun. When a prince was born in the royal household, a portion of the heavenly spirit entered into him. Should he never come to rule this spirit had no special power; the prince was in nature a man as other men are. But the moment he succeeded to the throne this spirit asserted itself, and he was raised as far above his subjects as were the gods they worshipped. Indeed, after his death, the King was honoured as a god, and his statue was placed among those of the gods in the temple.

Although the King had many names, he was too divine for the people to speak of him by any of his sovereign titles, so they invented some general name

The People of Ancient Egypt 15

and always used that instead. One of the commonest was the name Pharaoh, meaning "the great house in which all men live," or, "the great one who gives life to his people."

When not leading his armies in war, the King was occupied in dispensing justice and conducting religious festivals in the capital. What little leisure he had he loved to spend in hunting, and then would bid his artists picture him standing in his chariot and slaying the lions and other wild beasts that infested the surrounding desert.

Next in rank to the King was the Queen, who was supposed to be equal in rule with her husband. But it seldom happened that she was so, her quieter nature causing her to lead a more secluded life, and therefore bringing her less before the people. At times, however, a queen arose who made herself a power in the land. Of two such you are to read in this book.

The royal princes were given the chief offices of state. Some were made generals in the army, others priests, and others governors of the provinces into which Egypt was divided. There they lived in almost regal state, imitating in all things the life of the king at Court.

Next in rank were the great nobles and warriors, who were a specially privileged class, for they were each given a tract of land free of all taxes in return for their military services. The greater among them also received large revenues for the fulfilment of their duties as officers of state and of the King's army.

Of almost equal social importance and of far greater power were the priests, the learned class of the country. They alone knew the sacred rites, the mysteries, the ceremonials that their religion demanded, and that formed such a large part of their daily life. None but the King dare speak against the word of the High-priest, lest he should invoke upon the insolent one the wrath of the gods. And, with a people whose every action was guided by their faith in the gods, such a calamity must be averted at all costs. It was to maintain their influence over the people, by cultivating in them a sense of fear begotten of superstition, that the priests slowly introduced into the religion so much that was foreign to it, making a true and earnest faith an object of mockery to the nations around.

In the hands of the priests all records were kept, not only of matters touching their religion, but also of all events in the history of the nation. These were written on a substance prepared from the fibre of the papyrus plant, a long broad reed that grew abundantly among the marshes of the delta. Strips of fibre were laid side by side, and others placed at right angles across them, and the whole was made into a compact sheet by running between the fibres a kind of liquid gum. These sheets were about fourteen inches wide and of varying length, and when one sheet was filled, another was fastened to the end and the story continued, until

The People of Ancient Egypt 17

often the papyrus strip had grown to many yards in length. When all was finished, the papyrus was rolled up and stored away.

The writing was what is known as picture-writing, that is, drawings of objects—men and beasts and birds and plants—representing different ideas. From these pictures they afterward formed a phonetic alphabet, that is, the pictures represented certain sound values, so that they could write down ideas for which they had no separate picture. These were the forms adopted by the earliest architects, and on the ancient relics of the land these strange devices are to be found, graven deeply into the face of the stone. Because these carvings were done under the direction of the priests and used at first only for recording sacred knowledge, they are called "hieroglyphics," that is, sacred inscriptions carved in stone.

You will easily understand that this was a very slow process of writing, and so another was invented, which was a shortened form of the hieroglyphic. As this was used only by the priests it was called "hieratic," meaning priestly writing. A still more abridged form was invented later for the use of the people, or such as could read and write, and was called "demotic," or, the people's writing. In the British Museum, at the entrance of the large Egyptian gallery, is a broken slab of black stone on which are graven many strange characters; they are the text of an ancient Egyptian law written in hieroglyphic, demotic, and

Greek. It was the discovery of this stone about one hundred years ago that enabled men to begin the study of the hieroglyphics on stone and papyrus when the key to the riddle had for over a thousand years been lost.

The other classes of people were the artisans, the farmers, and the swineherds. The artisans formed guilds according to their crafts, and it was through the head man of the guild that they presented petitions to the King's officers. The farmers were the tillers of the soil, a hard-worked, often heavily-taxed body of men. But heavy taxes were the lot of most of the workers, who had to toil early and late to earn a bare living after the tax-gatherer had taken his toll.

Yet his hard life and many burdens did not make him brood, and at night, when at length he could lay aside his tools, the Egyptian loved to meet with his friends and talk and laugh over the events of the day, or sing a jovial song as the cup passed round. It was only gross injustice that made him groan in sorrow, and then he always had a remedy in the right to appeal to the highest officers, or, at stated times, to the King himself.

The houses of the artisans and farmers were built of wattles and mud, or of sun-dried bricks, such as may be seen in any Egyptian village to-day. Sometimes they had but one large room, but those of the more well-to-do often contained four or five rooms. There was little furniture, and that of the simplest kind. A rough wooden table, a few stone blocks that served

The People of Ancient Egypt 19

as seats, and a bed of woven reeds and fibre were the chief articles to be found.

The nobles and the wealthy people were much more favoured. Their houses were usually built of stone, well shaped and put together, and surrounded by large gardens wherein grew the choicest flowers, and fountains flashed and sparkled in the sun. Everything was present to minister to their comfort and happiness, and their palaces formed a striking contrast to the houses of their poorer brethren. But their luxuries did not make them heedless of the sterner duties of life, and it was among them that was found the true life of Egypt, the life that made her the greatest nation of ancient times, and the wonder of succeeding ages.

CHAPTER II
The Beliefs of the Egyptians

IN the book of the Bible called Exodus we read that Moses and Aaron went to Pharaoh, and in the name of the Lord God demanded that he should let the Israelites go to keep their feast in the wilderness. "And Pharaoh said," continues the narrative, "'Who is the Lord, that I should obey his voice to let Israel go ? I know not the Lord, neither will I let Israel go.'"

From such passages as this men formed the idea that the ancient Egyptians were a heathen people, worshippers of idols and images of stone, dealers in witchcraft, allies of the Prince of Darkness. But nothing could be further from the truth. They had a firm belief in a Supreme God, who overlooked their every act, and to whom they would have to account for every deed and thought in life. Nothing, not even the simplest action of daily work, would be undertaken without first calling on him in one of his many aspects to guide them in it aright.

By a careful study of the texts on tomb and papyrus, something of the truth about their ideas of an after-life

The Beliefs of the Egyptians

has at last been revealed. There are many sacred writings that tell of these ideas, but the one that gives us a better and fuller knowledge of their thoughts than any other is that known as the Book of the Dead. Its Egyptian name really means the "Coming Forth by Day," and it describes the journey of the spirit after death through the underworld, the trials and dangers it will encounter, and the means of overcoming them. The whole or parts of this book, often beautifully painted on papyrus, were placed in the tomb with the corpse; the more there was included the easier would it be for the spirit to traverse the gloomy regions below, and emerge at dawn upon the farther side with the sun-god to enter the "Fields of Peace."

But in this book that tells so much of their beliefs the name of their gods is legion, and we should be bewildered by their number if we did not know how they grew to be. The oldest portions of the sacred writings, put down some six thousand years ago, tell of an almighty Creator, the source and life of all things. But as the people could not understand how one Being, albeit a God, could possess the countless qualities ascribed to him, an explanation was furnished by the priests, who said the different attributes were so many different gods, each having a separate existence, and often acting independently of the rest. Thus the gods of the Egyptians became a vast army, whose purpose and duties could not be understood by other nations, nor even by the Egyptians themselves. But the priests and the learned people knew that these gods were only aspects of the different powers of the one great God, in whom and through whom they had their being.

The greatest of the gods was the Sun-God, Ra. Every morning he appeared on the eastern horizon, victorious from his fight with the powers of darkness, and began his daily journey in his boat called Millions of Years. On his way he looked down upon his people and saw their deeds of good and evil, and gave them light and heat, the sources of all life and power. In the evening he passed beyond the mountain of the west and dipped down into the Underworld, along whose dark and fearsome stream he went, crushing down the countless enemies that strove to stay him, and carrying along in his boat the souls of those who had successfully passed the judgment-hall of Osiris. Just as dawn broke he issued forth, to begin anew his journey across the heavens.

Thus in his daily course he overcame darkness, cloud and mist; and thence the Egyptians formed the moral idea of the conquest of truth over falsehood, of right over wrong. It was this conquest of which the sun was the emblem.

The centre of his worship was Heliopolis in the Delta, whence it spread until it embraced every town in Egypt. When in after days Amen, the god of Thebes, became more important, Ra did not fall from power in the eyes of the people; his powers were united with those of Amen and the god of Thebes was spoken of as Amen-Ra.

The Beliefs of the Egyptians   23

This god is usually depicted in human form, sometimes with the head of a man, sometimes with that of a hawk.

The god Amen was at first worshipped under this name only at Thebes, but his glory spread until he was acknowledged in all the lands of the north and the south, and hymns and praises were sung to him daily in every town and city of Egypt. The origin of their belief in this god is lost in the dark and misty beginnings of the race. His name means the Hidden One, and it is probable that he was the first god of whom the Egyptians had any clear ideas, the great original from whose various attributes sprang all the other gods. Long ages before writing was invented, prayer and praise were offered to him by this people. They believed in the existence of an eternal, almighty, all-wise Being, who could be neither seen nor known of man, yet who watched over him and was ever ready to hearken to his prayers; and slowly, as their ideas grew and strengthened, they put down in writing the picture they had formed of him. Part of a hymn that was sung daily in the great temple devoted to him at Thebes will show you something of this:

God is One and Alone, and there is none other beside Him.
God is one and Alone, the Maker of all His creatures.
God is a Spirit, deep-hidden from eye of man and from all things;

*God is the Spirit of Spirits, of Egypt the Spirit divine.
God is God from the beginning; before all things
   were He was God:
Lord of existences is He, Father of all, God Eternal.
God is the One Everlasting, Perpetual, Eternal,
   Unending;
From endless time hath He been, and shall be hence-
   forth and for ever.
God is Hidden, and no man His form hath per-
   ceived nor His likeness,
Unknown of Gods and of men, Mysterious, Incom-
   prehensible.
God is Truth, and on Truth doth He live; King of
   Truth divine is He.
God is Life; and man liveth through Him, the
   Primeval, alone.*

Of other gods the one most widely worshipped w
Osiris, the god who came down from heaven in the fo
of man to teach the people the arts of peace and to li
together in brotherly love. His brother Set or Typh
hated him bitterly and secretly murdered him. The
upon Isis his spouse set out to find him, and by l
divine power restored him to life. Horus, their son,
growing to manhood, marched against Typhon, and af
many encounters defeated him in a battle in the Del
This story, which was the one great legend loved of
the people, is set out at length in the succeeding pag(

For his sufferings and the wrongs he had undergo

The God Thoth

The Beliefs of the Egyptians 25

Osiris was chosen by the other gods to be Judge of the Dead, and there, deep in the Underworld he sat, waiting every night to pronounce judgment on the souls that had passed with Ra into the Valley of the Shadow of Death.

Another God of great reverence was Thoth. He represented the Divine intelligence, and so became the god of wisdom and learning. In pictures of the judgment-scene before Osiris, he stands beside the balance in which the heart of man was weighed, tablet and reed in hand, waiting to record the result. For this reason he was also spoken of as the Recorder. In paintings he is depicted with the head of an ibis, above which was the crescent moon to show he was also the measurer of time.

Of the other gods little need be said. Kheper-Ra was only a special name given to Ra, on his rising in the east. Nephthys, the sister of Isis, was a deity of the dead. Anubis, a deity of the third order, son of Osiris and Isis, was the ruler of graves. Set, the brother of Osiris, was regarded as the chief power of evil. He was at first looked upon as a friendly god; but as the legend grew of his struggle with Osiris and his final vanquishment by Horus, he became the type of evil and the enemy of man, just as Horus became the Saviour of mankind.

A peculiarity of the Egyptian beliefs was that the gods often visited earth to watch the doings of man, when they entered into the bodies of different animals. Hence almost all animals were looked upon as sacred to one or other of the gods, the scarab or beetle to Kheper-Ra, the jackal to Anubis, the ibis to Thoth; and to kill any creature proclaimed as sacred was a crime punished by death, though, were it done unwittingly, the priest might cause a fine to be paid instead. Each kind was tended by appointed guardians, their food being provided from offerings of the people when they came to temple-worship. After death their bodies were carefully buried, sometimes being embalmed and sent to particular cities where they were buried in a temple, as at Bubastis, where was a temple-tomb for cats.

The most sacred of all animals was the cow, honoured as the emblem of the goddess Hat-hor. The bull was also an object of special worship, for he was sacred to Osiris, Judge of the Dead. The Apis Bull, as he was called, was carefully chosen by the priests in accordance with certain marks which he must possess. His hide was black, and on his forehead was a white triangular spot; the hair on his back was arranged in the form of an eagle, and on his right side was a white mark like to the crescent moon; while under his tongue was the symbol of the sacred scarab. When this animal was found, a day of public rejoicing was proclaimed, and throughout the length and breadth of the land men feasted in his honour.

When he was able to be taken from his mother, the Apis bull was led by priests and wise men down to the river and conducted in a gilded barge to Memphis, where was a special temple built for him, with court-

The Beliefs of the Egyptians

yards, gardens, and fountains; and there he remained the rest of his life. Every year on the anniversary of his birth, a great festival was held; and when he died the whole land went into mourning for him, which lasted until another Apis was found. His body was embalmed and buried, but none of those in attendance on him was allowed to reveal the place of burial. Only a few years ago this spot was discovered, a great temple hewn out of the rock, its passages lined with chambers in each of which was a great stone sarcophagus, the final resting-place of the animal that had received so much honour and worship in life.

A few animals, like the pig, were regarded as unclean, and with these none but the swineherds would have anything to do. Did a man but touch one with the skirt of his robe in passing, he hurried straight away to the river and plunged in, clothes and all, to wash away the pollution.

Snakes and serpents were generally considered evil and destroyed; the greatest enemy the soul had to encounter in the Underworld was figured in their religious books as an enormous serpent, named Apepi. But a few kinds were sacred, one, the uraeus or basilisk, being held in deep veneration. Its image was carved over the gateway of nearly every temple in Egypt, and, wrought in gold, it formed the chief ornament of the Egyptian crown.

Many kinds of birds, too, were holy, the chief being the hawk and the ibis, a bird of a white plumage with long black tail, and with legs like a stork. The hawk was sacred to Horus, and the ibis to Thoth. If anyone killed either of these birds, accidentally or otherwise, he was punished by death.

Thus the ancient Egyptian had a firm and well-arranged belief in the presence of God in all the creatures about him; and in the rewards and punishments to be meted out to him hereafter in accordance with his deeds, be they good or bad, while on earth. This belief in an after-life was the mainspring of all his thoughts and actions. Nothing was entered upon without consulting the gods, nor carried through without the knowledge that they were watching him in all he did. He led, therefore, a highly moral life, and his teachings are of the noblest and purest character.

Moreover, he believed not only that the soul would pass to heaven, but that the body too would rise to continue its existence in a more perfect world. To this end it behoved him to take the utmost care in its preservation after death, that it might be ready when the soul should return to claim it. The dead body was sent to men specially instructed in embalming, who, by means of aromatics and mysterious drugs, so treated it that it was proof against decay. Their skill is shown in the many mummies, as we call them, to be seen in our museums to-day, often as lifelike after thousands of years as they were when first laid to rest.

After being embalmed the body of a king or great noble was laid in a beautiful granite sarcophagus,

The Beliefs of the Egyptians

whose sides were carved with pictures of the journey of the dead through the underworld. About the tomb were placed statues of the gods who were the special protectors of the dead, and the walls were covered with sacred texts, painted in glowing colours, to help the soul on its way. Those who could not afford such costly burials had coffins made of wood, on which was painted, in addition to the sacred words, the portrait of the dead. This is the sort of coffin usually seen in the museums. But were it granite or wood, or merely the friendly desert sand that enclosed the mortal remains, it mattered little. There the body waited, in a calm and tranquil peace, for the return of the soul from its wanderings and struggles, when again they would be reunited ; and, filled with the spirit of purity and truth, would wend their way to the realms that were called the " Fields of Perfect Peace."

CHAPTER III
The Beginning of All Things

LONG ages ago, more thousands of years than you could count, there was neither earth nor sea nor sky. Nothing but one vast watery mass stretched through all space, and thus it had been from all eternity. In this mass lived God, the Spirit that had always existed with it, but he had no form, nor shape, nor actual being; and in the fluid itself there was no life, no movement, nothing to indicate that out of it one day should spring our beautiful world and its canopy of star-studded sky.

Then it happened that this Spirit who lived within the waters was moved to utter his name, and the action brought him into being in the form of God, a grand majestic figure, from whom afterward sprang all the other gods, men and women, animals and plants, and everything that was created. His name was Khepera, that is, he who becomes the light and life of all things; and there, in solitary dignity, he brooded over the face of the deep.

As yet Khepera had no place whereon to stand, so, after deep meditation, he resolved to separate the

The Beginning of All Things 31

substances of which the fluid mass was composed, and from them he made the earth and the sea. Then he thought it would be desirable to have other gods to work with him, and, by the power of his word, he created two helpers, one of whom became the source of light and the other the sky that overhung the earth like a big blue curtain.

Now, although there was a god of light, there was nothing yet made to distinguish light from darkness. So one day the new gods brought to Khepera a great fiery ball, and this he took and put in his head for an eye. So brightly did it shine that it lighted up the whole earth, on which it looked down to see all that was done as it travelled daily across the sky. For this eye was none other than the sun; and, because it not only was the source of all light and heat, and so of all life on earth, but also could see everything that happened and nothing could be hidden from it, in later ages men looked upon it, too, as a god, the greatest god of all.

Once when Ra, for that was the name of the eye, returned from his travels across the sky to report to the great Spirit what he had seen, he found that Khepera had got another eye. True, this was not so powerful as Ra, but none the less he was very angry. He may have thought that his supreme position as Lightgiver was endangered; at the best his kingdom was to be shared with another. Filled with jealousy he raged against the Creator, and Khepera, perhaps to punish him, ordained that the new eye not only should give light when Ra was not present in the sky, but also should be called the measurer of time. That is why the moon has been used by all people to reckon the length of the month.

So far nothing had been made but that which should assist Khepera in his work. But now he resolved to fill the earth with creatures who should worship him. First of all he created six more gods, each of whom had special duties allotted to him, and who in after days received due homage from mankind; then from his tears were fashioned men and women, whom he put upon the earth. That they might find pleasure in life he made the trees and plants and grasses and all manner of green things that grow. Then he made the reptiles, birds, and animals; and, having thus satisfied the needs of man, the Creator rested from his work. And that is how all things began.

CHAPTER IV

The Life Beyond

I. THE HEAVEN OF THE EGYPTIANS

TO the earliest dwellers in the Nile valley the earth was not such as we know it to be. It was a long narrow valley surrounded by lofty mountains, that rose in the north to a very great height.

Above the earth was the ceiling of the sky, which, said some, was the face of a man, the sun and moon being his eyes, while his long flowing hair formed pillars to support the roof. Most people, however, conceived the sky as a canopy of iron, " the heavenly metal," held up by four towering peaks in the encircling mountains in the north and south and east and west. High up on the mountain slopes was a broad ledge on which ran the celestial Nile, traversing a vast semicircle from east to west. Along this stream was carried the boat of the Sun-god Ra, known as the boat of Millions of Years, and so long as Ra was in his boat light was given to the earth. In the evening when he reached Manu, the mountain of the west, where the heavenly Nile poured down into a deep abyss behind the mountain range, he passed from sight, and did not reappear until morning, when he emerged near Bakhu, the mount of the east, to repeat his journey, and to shed his bounties on the earth below.

When the river disappeared at sunset, the Sun-god did not continue in his boat, although his spirit accompanied it in its journeyings. Ra passed on to the roof that overcovered the earth, where was the home of the gods and goddesses and those of mankind who had gained admission into heaven. For this was the heaven they sought to attain to, the land they called the Fields of Peace. Here, seated on a magnificent throne that was ornamented with the heads of lions and the feet of bulls, emblems both of majesty and strength, the mighty Ra dispensed justice, and directed all things in heaven and earth. Around his throne, seated or standing, were the gods of his train, ready to carry out his commands at a nod or a sign from their lord.

Then there were the other great gods, many of whom were scarcely less powerful than Ra himself, each with a number of attendants chosen from the heavenly hosts. Again, far removed in grandeur from these powerful divinities, but equally distant from those they had left behind, were those of mankind who had passed through the valley of the shadow of death, and who, by the help of friendly gods, and the merit of their good deeds on earth, had come forth on the other side, to be admitted to the lands of the blessed.

This land, Aalu, as it was called, was not such a heaven as many early nations have pictured to themselves: there were no shining mansions, no streets of gold, no gorgeous buildings adorned with countless precious jewels. The life hereafter that the Egyptian thought of was but a continuation of his life on earth, without its pains and sorrows. His heaven, therefore, consisted of fertile lands, traversed by endless canals, whose water came from the celestial stream itself. Here grew white wheat and red barley in plenty, the vine and the figtree supplied him with fruit; and spreading sycamores yielded ample shade when the heaven-dweller wished to rest.

Yet it was no life of idle ease that he conceived. He had to plough, and sow, and reap, and thresh, just as he had done before. But between this life and that to come was one great difference. There the work was light, and the worker was free from the cares that often beset him here. He need never be anxious about an excessive flood, against which the earthly Nile would keep him struggling for life day and night, nor fear a day when the Nile would yield no water, and his land would be scorched by the burning rays of the sun. Against these and other like calamities that had harassed him heretofore, the gods made due provision; everything was well ordered by them, and care was unknown.

Not all the earthborn attained to heavenly happiness. Some were unworthy, and many of the weak fell by the way when passing through the dark valley. Only when strengthened by the merit of noble deeds on earth, by respect and honour paid to the gods, and by careful preparation for the long journey after death, could man hope to arrive at last at the Fields of Perfect Peace.

II. THE UNDERWORLD OF THE EGYPTIANS

You have read how the celestial Nile disappeared at the mountain called Manu into a vast abyss, and issued forth again at that called Bakhu. Between these two peaks the boat of the Sun-god Ra was hidden from sight, for there he passed through the region called Tuat, the place to which went all the spirits of men and women when the body was claimed by death.

The chief part of the Tuat was a deep valley called Amentet. It was in the form of a semicircle, the sides of which were rocky and precipitous; and along the bottom ran the heavenly stream which fell over the edge of Manu. There reigned eternal night; and from the black and turbid waters arose such foul vapours that no human being could breathe them and live. Horrors of every kind infested the whole course of the river, and the place would terrify the stoutest of heart. Yet over this awful pathway the soul must pass before it could enter into heaven.

The Tuat was divided into twelve regions, each corresponding to an hour of the night. The entrance to each was protected by massive walls and doors, and guarded by terrible snakes. Snakes and serpents of enormous length lay coiled on the rocks bordering the river, waiting to seize the pilgrim who was not properly equipped for his voyage. Sometimes hanging down from the cliffs above, they caught the unwary traveller and crushed him in their mighty folds; again they hovered over the very brink of the river, and belched forth fire to consume the passers-by. .

Clearly the soul of itself could not hope to go through all these perils unharmed. So every night the company of those who had died gathered together at the mouth of Amentet, and, as the boat of Ra entered the world of gloom, they crowded around it to be taken on board. Many succeeded in climbing in; many more, those who were not duly prepared, were seized by the loathly reptiles, or fell into the inky waters, where they became a prey to the huge crocodiles that inhabited their depths.

Those who had been fortunate enough to get on board the Boat of Millions of Years were now under the protection of Ra. This, however, did not free them from anxiety, and they had still to fight against the enemies that thronged the river and its banks, ready to overturn the boat and destroy its occupants. Often the battle was fierce and long; but, strengthened by the arm of Ra, and the magical words and the prayers he had learned, the soul overcame each enemy in turn.

Thus did the spirit-host thread the first five divisions of the Tuat, in each of which Ra was acknowledged supreme god. Then, in the middle of the night, the boat arrived at the sixth division, the most awesome of all.

For this was the Hall of Osiris, Judge of the Dead, through which the soul could pass only by virtue of good deeds wrought when on earth. Here even the might of Ra was powerless to aid him. Great and irresistible as the Sun-god was elsewhere, in the realms of Osiris he had no place. From them he was shut out, and the soul must stand alone.

At the far end of a mighty hall, on a splendid golden throne approached by nine broad steps, sat the dread judge. In his hand he held the sceptre, and on his head was the double crown of the two Egypts. On either side stood Isis, and Nephthys, his wife and sister; before him knelt Anubis, the god who presided over the balance in which the heart of man was weighed; and Thoth, the scribe of the gods, stood by to record the result of the weighing. Forty-two gods on thrones of ivory and gold were ranged around the hall. Just behind the balance, under the very steps of Osiris's throne, yawned a fathomless pit, at the back of which there grinned a fearsome monster, ready to devour all that was thrown therein.

In sooth the soul might well shrink with fear as he entered the awful chamber; but little time was allowed for thought. Anon the forty-two gods began to question him, and to their questions he must reply satisfactorily or be driven out into everlasting darkness. "Hast thou been guilty of theft?" said one. "Hath thy tongue spoken falsely against thy neighbour?" asked another. "Hast thou taken the life of

The Life Beyond

thy brother?" questioned a third. "Didst thou honour the gods?" "Didst thou love thy neighbour as thyself?" And thus the examination went on. But by means of the knowledge gained from sacred writings the soul knew how to reply to each one in turn, and at length the gods were satisfied.

But the most trying part of the ordeal was yet to come. As the examination came to an end, Horus, son of Osiris, and special guardian of the souls of the Underworld, came forward, and, taking the spirit-man by the hand, presented him to the Judge of the Dead. His heart was placed in one pan of the balance, and in the other a feather, the emblem of truth. There the soul stood, watching in fear and trembling the swing of the balance, and shuddering with horror as his eye fell on the nameless pit, where the beast sat greedily watching too. For here no subterfuge could avail. It was eternal and unchanging Truth against which he was being weighed. If the scale with his heart proved the heavier, or even if it just balanced the feather on the other side, he was accepted of Osiris. But woe to him whose heart proved light! Tears and lamentations profited him nothing. He was seized by the attendants of the gods, and cast to destruction into the pit where the monster waited for his prey.

The successful soul, accepted of Osiris, was now led out of the judgment hall, and again entered the boat of Ra in the seventh division of the Tuat. From this point the journey was much easier, for, strengthened by the knowledge of his own goodness, the soul could overcome the foes that beset his path. But the darkest hour is that before the dawn; and for the pilgrim there was one more danger to pass. In the twelfth division of the Tuat the boat of Ra was faced by a serpent of such enormous size that it filled the entire channel of the stream; and, as the boat could not sail round it, nor pass over it, it must needs go *through* it. Black as had been the voyage before, it was as naught compared to the thick darkness now; and even here, on the very threshold of a new world, the soul might have been lost but for the protecting power of Ra.

At length a faint gleam of light appeared, that rapidly grew brighter and brighter. Then the last great door burst open, and to welcoming songs of triumph from the choirs of gods and spirits above, the Boat of Millions of Years emerged into the full light of day. And, as the Sun-god cast his beams wide over the earth, the crowd of those whom he brought in his train joined in the strain of praise, a hymn that echoed loud across the vault of heaven as they were received into the Lands of Perfect Peace.

CHAPTER V
The Story of Ra and Isis

IN those far distant days before history begins, it is said that there lived in Egypt a woman of great knowledge called Isis. She was well skilled in all arts and magic, and her wisdom and learning were equal to those of the gods. This superiority over her fellow-creatures made her desirous of yet more power and honour. " Why should I not," she said to herself, " make myself mistress of all the earth, and become like unto a goddess in heaven ? Did I know the secret name of Ra, verily I could accomplish this."

Now when Ra, the greatest of the gods, was created, his father had given him a secret name, so awful that no man dared to seek for it, and so pregnant with power that all the other gods desired to know and possess it too. That they might not find it out by spells and enchantments it was hidden within the body of the Sun-god himself. But what man dared not, and the gods had failed to do, Isis resolved to achieve.

Every morning Ra came forth from the land of darkness and travelled across the sky in his Boat of

Millions of Years. Now Isis had noticed that water fell from his mouth; so she took some of this and the earth on which it had fallen and fashioned them in the form of a sacred serpent, which, by reason of its being made from the spittle of a god, came to life when she uttered over it one of her magic spells. The serpent she then laid carefully in the path of Ra, in such wise that he should not see it and yet he must pass over it. Thus, indeed, it fell out. On his next journey as he passed by the place where the serpent lay hid, the reptile bit him. The pain was intense, and Ra began to cry aloud. "What is it?" asked the gods who attended on him. "Wherefore criest thou thus as if in pain?" But Ra found no words wherewith to answer them. His limbs shook, his teeth chattered, his face became pale, and his whole body was rapidly being suffused with the poison.

At length the Sun-god called his companions to him. "Come hither, ye gods," he cried, "and hear what hath befallen me. I have been bitten by something deadly. My eyes have not seen it, nor did I make it: it is not one of my creatures. But never have I felt pain so mortal. I am God, the son of God, and I was travelling through my lands to see them and my people, when the creature arose in my path and wrought me this ill. Go quickly, therefore, to the other gods, and bring those who are skilled in spells and enchantments that they may take away this pain."

Soon the company of the gods, especially those versed

The Story of Ra and Isis

in the use of magical words, were assembled about the boat of Ra; and with them came the woman Isis. In vain did Ra's companions use their talismans and utter their spells; the poison continued to burn within him. Then Isis approached, and said, "What is this, O Ra? Surely some serpent hath bitten thee; some one of thy creatures hath dared to raise its head against the hand that made it. Tell me thy name, I pray thee, thy secret name, that by its power I may cast out the poison and thou shalt be whole."

"I am the maker of heaven and earth," answered Ra, "and without me was nothing made that is made. When I open my eye, behold, it is light; and when I close it again, then darkness reigns. My word brings the flood into the Nile to water the land of Egypt. I make the hours, the days, and the yearly festivals. I am he who was, and is, and ever shall be."

"Verily thou hast told me who thou art," said Isis, "but not yet hast thou spoken thy secret name. Wouldst thou be healed, thou must divulge it to me, that by its power and my lore I may overcome the evil wrought unto thee."

Meanwhile the poison was coursing through the body of Ra, and making him very ill indeed; for you must remember that the serpent was a magic serpent, and also that it had not been created by Ra himself; for which reasons, though he was the greatest of the gods, he could not destroy the effects of its venom. One moment his body burnt as with fire, and the next it was icy cold, as the fever raged through and through him. Finally he could no longer stand, and he sank down in the boat.

Then he called Isis to him. "I consent," he said to the company around him, "I consent to be searched out by Isis, and that my name be yielded up unto her." So Ra and Isis went apart, lest the assembled gods should also overhear the secret name, and Ra confessed that which the woman so greatly longed to know.

As soon as she had obtained her wish, Isis began to utter her magic spells, and here her ancient wisdom stood her in good stead. Then she cried aloud, "Come out, poison, depart from the body of Ra. Let Ra live! May Ra live! Poison, depart from the body of Ra." At the words a change came over the mighty god. No longer did he seem about to die. Quickly his strength returned, and ere long he was whole again, ready to continue his journey in the Boat of Millions of Years. And Isis, who by her wit had learnt what neither man nor god ever knew, was granted her desire, and henceforth was known as the mistress of the gods.

What was the secret name, do you ask? Ah! that I cannot tell you. It is what wise men have been seeking for thousands of years. Some few have found it, but the strange thing is that no one can tell it to anyone else. He can help others on the way to discover it for themselves, but that is all; and very often people neglect to hear it when it is whispered to them.

The Story of Ra and Isis

They let it pass, borne away on the wings of the wind, and the opportunity comes not again. But to those who do find out the secret name, it is all-sufficient They need nothing more, for it is the greatest gift that heaven or earth can bestow.

The Story of Isis and Osiris

CHAPTER VI

The Kingdom of Osiris

I. THE BIRTH OF THE GOD

FAR up the river Nile, on a fertile strip of land that borders the stream, once stood the mighty city of Thebes. Its ruins still cover a large area, and in the days of its greatest splendour it was the most magnificent city in the world. But at the time when this story opens, it was still young, and its gorgeous temples were not yet built. Its people worshipped, it is true, but not the God of Heaven. Amen they knew not, and the majesty of Ra they could not have understood. Their gods were images of wood and stone and the sun and the river Nile.

To these false gods a temple had been built, on a site destined to become the centre of a grand and noble worship. It stood amid a grove of shady trees, and from under its portals bubbled forth a spring of purest water, so sweet and sparkling that the people said it was blessed by the gods they honoured there.

To this spring a water-carrier was trudging one hot summer morning. He was young, but already his back was bowed with constant stooping under the weight of his goatskin bag.

"Why work at this hour?" asked a brother carrier, who, with goatskin slung over his shoulder, was wending homeward.

"Why work at all, I might ask," replied the other sourly.

"True, but 'needs must,' you know," said the first. "Otherwise, methinks neither of us would be here now. Yet to-day is different. With this fierce heat blowing off the desert one cannot be blamed for resting early. It might do thee good," he went on, seeing the other did not speak. "Thou dost not seem in merry mood."

"Nor do I feel so," was the curt reply. "But one must eat; and such as I cannot eat unless he works. There are many to feed now, for my father lies ill, and I must needs provide for all."

"Well, I shall wait until evening; 'twill be cooler then," said his companion as he walked away.

Pamyles, for such was the water-carrier's name, watched his friend depart, and felt bitter in his heart against the fate that had made his lot so hard. Then, remembering the hungry mouths in the little hut of reeds by the river, he turned to the spring.

Just as he had filled the skin, he thought he heard his name called. He looked round, but saw no one. "Pamyles," came the voice again. There could be no doubt about it this time, and he paused in lifting the water-bag to stare at the steps leading up to the temple. "Pamyles," came the voice a third time; and the poor man, knowing not what might befall him, dropped the goatskin to the ground, where the water gushed out unheeded, making a pool about his feet.

"Fear not," said the voice, which to Pamyles's astonished senses seemed to come from the statue before the temple-door. "Fear not; but go down into the town and say to the people, 'Osiris, lord of all the earth, is born.' Afterwards proclaim the message throughout the length and breadth of the land."

The voice ceased, and, on the instant, Pamyles, forgetting all about the water-skin, took to his heels and never stopped until he reached his house. There he told the story to his wife, who said the heat had muddled his wits, and bade him go back for the goatskin before some one came and stole it. But the old man, his sire, who lay with eyes closed on a bed of straw at the farther end of the room, called his son to him and asked him to repeat his tale.

"It was the voice of heaven," said the old man, as Pamyles concluded. "Go proclaim thy message as thou hast been bidden. For myself, I rejoice that I have lived to hear the gladsome tidings. May the blessing of the gods be upon thee, my son." And the sufferer turned his face to the wall, and died.

Then Pamyles hastened to do as he had been commanded; and thus it was that the news of Osiris's birth came to the world.

II. THE COMING OF THE GOD AND GODDESS

One evening in early summer, as the westering sun hung over the hills in a sea of crimson and purple and gold, a man halted under a sycamore tree near a rude temple that overlooked the Nile at Thebes. He was of enormous stature, yet so properly formed withal that one would scarce have heeded it until another man stood beside him. Then he seemed more than mortal.

By his side stood a woman, surely the most beautiful and most graceful on whom the sun had ever risen. The sweet and gentle face, fair of skin and tinted rosy-red, the comely figure clad in a robe of clinging white, and the wealth of chestnut hair that, when it fell down to her feet, covered her as with a garment and shone in the dying sunlight like burnished copper, told of a traveller from other lands than the burning plains of Egypt. As the sun's disk dipped behind the peak, changing the dull grey and brown of the hills to deepest purple, and painting the waters of the river in flaming red, she turned to the man and then toward the setting orb. Lifting their hands in adoration, they called on the name of Ra, bowed thrice to the ground, and sang a short hymn in the Sun-god's praise.

"Let us tarry here and rest," said the man, and, spreading his mantle on a slab of stone, they sat down; when he took from his cloak a reed and began to blow upon it. Was it possible that this music was born of earth? Now soft as the cooing of the doves in the

The Coming of Osiris and Isis

trees, now plaintive as a sea-bird's call; anon rippling like a stream over the pebbles in its bed, then loud and fast even as the rushing of a mountain torrent, it ended at last with such a burst of swelling sound as comes from a mighty choir that sings in unison. Then he played a simple song to the chant of the woman's voice. Wonderful had been the playing; marvellous beyond all words was the singing! Soft and low, yet thrilling in its richness and fulness, it seemed to tell of joy and sorrow, of brightness and shadow, of storm and sunshine, and of an infinity of love.

As the last sweet strains died away, a venerable old man, clad in a white robe encircled by a belt of gold, came slowly toward the two wayfarers.

"A pleasant even to you both," he said, a mixture of awe and wonder plainly written on his face.

"And to thee, O my father," said the man. "Canst tell us," he asked, "where in this city we may find lodging for a time? We are travellers, and would fain stay here to rest awhile."

For some moments the newcomer said not a word, but continued to gaze with eyes that would read them through and through. At length he bowed his head to the ground, and kissed the sandal, first of the man then of the woman. Thereon, looking up, he spoke.

"The makers of music such as I have heard," he said, "should have the best the city can give. I am the priest of this temple, and in my study of the stars I have learned somewhat of the mysteries of the heavens.

Long have I known of your coming, but never did I think that I should be the first to greet you here on earth." And with worshipping eyes again the holy man gazed on the wondrous pair. " Will my lord and lady deign to accept such hospitality as my poor house can offer ? " he asked.

"It is because thou hast been so faithful in thy service that we came to thee first," replied the man. "We thank thee, and accept thy kindness. But I charge thee straitly to tell no man what thou knowest, whence we came or why. That shall be known as the gods will."

"Your servant hears, and obeys," said the priest, and he bowed his head to the dust.

"Now lead us to thy house," continued the stranger. "Come, Isis," he said, turning to the woman, "we will go with him, for the hour groweth late."

"The blessing of Ra be with thee alway," said the woman to the priest in her rich low voice ; and, placing her arm within the other's, they went forward.

And in this wise did Osiris and Isis his consort come to the land of Egypt.

III. THE POWER OF OSIRIS

Every day Osiris and Isis went into the town that lay in the shadow of the temple. The wealthy palaces, the sacred buildings, the sphinx-lined avenues, and all the marks of grandeur and power for which Thebes became famous, were then unknown. The king's palace and the residences of some few of his great nobles were built of stone; but for the most part the houses were built of wood and reeds, or of bricks of mud baked in the sun, such as may be seen in any village of Egypt to-day.

As the two passed through the streets, the people stopped their work to look on them in amaze. Never had such majesty, such dignity, such power been seen in any man; never such sweetness, grace, and loveliness in any woman. Even their king and queen seemed insignificant compared with these godlike creatures. Instinctively they felt that the strangers were not of earth, and every mark of respect was shown them by the simple folk.

As you may guess, there were numerous inquiries at the house of the priest concerning the guests that abode there. But the high priest kept his own counsel; and for the rest of his household, they knew no more than did the people themselves. "They are travellers," was their reply to every inquirer, "whom Ani the priest met in the temple grove and prayed to abide with him awhile. That is all we know." Which way had they come? Did they travel by boat or on asses? What had they come for? But to these and all other questions no answer was forthcoming. The mystery of their arrival only added to the awe in which the people held them.

As time passed by, this awe deepened into a worshipping fear. Day by day Osiris and Isis went among the people, advising, helping, cheering. Wherever they were most needed there they always seemed to be. No hand was so cooling to the fevered brow as that of Isis, no voice so soothing to the fretful child; and, what was most remarkable, the sickness of those whom she touched and nursed quickly left them. Once when a distracted mother sought to ease the pain of her little boy, crushed and broken by the falling of a log, she felt the mysterious lady beside her. Gently Isis took the sufferer in her arms, and, as if by magic, the contorted face grew straight, the writhing limbs were stilled. Then she placed the tips of her fingers on his brow, and, after a moment, over his heart. The eyes slowly opened, the lips smiled. The child's look wandered from the nurse to his mother, and back again. "Mother, mother," he cried suddenly, "I'm going with the beautiful lady. She says so, mother. I'm going to a beautiful house and I shall feel the pain no more." He died that night, but he did not suffer again, and the stricken mother understood.

Osiris, too, was ever busy, but it was in the fields rather than in the houses of the city. He showed them how to make a plough, and then a water-raiser to lift the water from the river for the thirsty soil instead of carrying it all on their backs. Much else after the same manner did he teach them, to lighten their labour and to use more fruitfully the land they tilled. In the cool of the evening he would sit, surrounded by a crowd of rustics, young and old, all open-mouthed with

The Kingdom of Osiris

admiration as he played to them upon his reed. Gradually he taught them how to play, too, and ofttimes would be found a choir of churls pouring forth harmonious music in the liquid moonlight. And his little court would never let him depart until he had played to them one favourite hymn, that breathed of earth and sky, of life and death, and of a multitude of things beyond their knowing.

It was not long before the king heard of the strangers in their midst, and he sent for Osiris to come before him.

"Who art thou?" he asked; "and whence comest thou?"

"I am a traveller," said Osiris, "who has heard much of the land of Egypt and desired to see it and its people. I came from the land of Aalu, and tarry here but a little while ere I return thither."

"Where is this land thou speakest of?" asked the king. "My armies have marched far and wide, but never have I heard of it before."

"It lieth far away to the West," replied Osiris, "beyond the utmost limits that man can travel, unless he have a guide."

"Then how didst thou come?" said the king. "If thou couldst come hither, I can go thither. Tell me the road, for I would see this distant land."

"That thou canst not do," said Osiris. "I have said that no man can reach it, so far away doth it lie."

"Then thou wilt never return to thy own land?" said the monarch.

"Not while I live," was the reply. "I shall set out on the journey, but I do not look to reach it while life lasteth."

"I have heard much of thy skill and cunning," continued the king. "I wish thee to come to my palace and teach my courtiers and magicians something of it."

"Willingly," answered Osiris. "Yet I cannot forgo my work amongst thy poor people, also the right to help them as I have done hitherto."

Thus it came to pass that Osiris went daily to the court, sitting with the wise men, who always learned something new from him. To all their entreaties, however, to take up his abode in the palace, he remained obdurate. He had every comfort in the house of the priest, he said, and would stay with the man who had first befriended him.

Often in his discourse with the people he would speak with them of the temple wherein they worshipped, telling them that the stone image before which they uttered their prayers was powerless to aid them; but watching over them was a Divine Being who shielded them from harm and furnished all their needs. The golden sun that brought light and heat was a visible manifestation of this Being's power and majesty; the river Nile that watered the land, giving nourishment to their crops, was sent by Him from out of heaven.

By living noble and unselfish lives it was possible even for men to attain to the country where the great God lived in splendour and glory. In this way Osiris slowly inspired in the people a sense of worship of the Supreme Being; the more easily because his own deeds were so miraculous that his hearers were more than half disposed to look upon him as the God of whom he spoke.

Among the courtiers assembled in the open courtyard of the king on a certain day of audience, Osiris noted, as he entered, a young man standing, silent and apart, and withal a look of settled gloom upon his face. He was a warrior who had won the heart of Osiris, because of his fearless bearing, his chivalrous conduct, and his cheerful frankness. Clearly something was amiss, and Osiris crossed to where he stood.

" What aileth thee, Hotep ? " he asked. " Why dost thou brood here apart, instead of making merry with thy friends ? "

" There is none will speak to me, or none who dares to," said the young man, somewhat bitterly. " Dost thou not know the king will visit thee with his displeasure doth he see thee with me now ? "

Osiris then observed that the courtiers were talking chiefly in whispers and ofttimes glancing significantly toward the youth. " What is thy fault ? " he said.

" That I have not flattered those in high places, nor held my peace in face of wrong," replied Hotep. " Thus have I made many enemies, who have accused me of plotting against the king's life, and he has bid me attend here to answer the charge."

"Ah!" exclaimed Osiris. "So there are those who envy thy fearlessness and truth!" And he slowly moved away to speak to the temple priest, his head bowed in thought.

At that moment the king entered, and the attention of the courtiers was taken up with the audiences given by him. At last all were over; but, instead of rising to leave the hall as was his wont, the monarch sat on in his chair of state.

"Is our servant Hotep here?" he asked at length.

"Here, O King," said the young man, stepping forward and making deep obeisance.

"We have received accusations against thy fidelity, that thou hast plotted against the royal throne," said the king. "Hast thou aught to say in answer to the charge?"

"I beg my lord to let me hear the charges more particularly," replied Hotep.

The monarch frowned. It was not usual for a subject to imply doubt of the king's word; but after a moment he called the chamberlain to him. "Read what the charges are," he said.

"Hotep thy servant, captain in the king's army, is accused of plotting against the life of the king and his royal house," recited the minister from the scroll in his hand, "and of inciting others to aid him in his villainous work. Further, in his capacity of captain of the army of the South, he hath sought to create disaffection in the ranks of the king's troops, purposing to use them to carry out his evil designs."

"What sayest thou to these accusations?" said the king, when the chamberlain had finished.

"Who are my accusers?" asked Hotep quietly.

Again the king's brow clouded. "It matters not," he said angrily. "Thou hast heard the charge. Hast thou aught to reply?"

"Nothing, O King, save that it is a base lie, fabricated by my enemies," said the fearless youth. "O King, thou knowest the faithfulness of my service, and I abide thy decision, trusting to the king's honour."

For a brief space the king was discomfited. Then his anger returned.

"The penalty for thy sin is death," he answered, "and thy guilt hath been proved. Take him away," he said, turning to the guards behind him.

The warrior darted a swift look round the hall. He was young, and life was sweet. But no answering glance met his in the crowd of faces about him. Whatever it was that passed through his mind he recognized the hopelessness of it, and, with a bitter smile, turned to the men who had come to lead him away.

"Doth the king condemn a man unheard?" said Osiris, who, unmarked, had advanced to the throne. "Is it to his honour or to his weal thus to send a well-tried servant to his death."

A gasp of deep amaze sounded like a sudden wind

through the hall. Never had anyone been known to question in this wise the will of the king. The monarch himself was for the moment too astounded to speak.

"Thou presumest too much on the favour I have shown thee," he said, when at length words came to him. "I have spoken. Were it not that thou art a stranger within our gates, thy rashness might have brought on thee the same punishment as his for whom thou speakest. Stand aside, and meddle no further, or it will be worse for thee."

"Nevertheless, I ask thee to give the man justice," said Osiris quietly. "Wouldst thou——"

"Darest thou speak thus to me?" roared the king in a fury. "Take this fool away too," he cried to the guards, "lest I kill him where he stands." And the long lance quivered in his hand.

"I move not until thou hast dealt justice to thy servant Hotep," answered Osiris, calm and unmoved as heretofore.

"Madman," shouted the king, "suffer for thy folly;" and he sprang forward, the lance poised to strike.

"Stand," said Osiris. And now his voice rolled through the hall like thunder amid far-echoing hills.

Paralysed at the word the monarch halted, and the lance clattered upon the granite floor. The courtiers stared in utter dread, marvelling what would next betide. A very god seemed Osiris, towering above them all as a man might over a crowd of little children, his arm outstretched, his eyes gleaming like the lightning.

Slowly he lowered his arm to his side; slowly the king recovered consciousness, and, shaking with terror, sank back into his seat.

"Hadst thou come one step more," said Osiris, "thou wouldst now be wending to the shades below. Know that I have power to destroy thee and all these assembled round thee. Now wilt thou set free thy servant Hotep, falsely accused, and mete out punishment to those who would accomplish his death. Rouse not my wrath again, but remember, and fear." And ere speech or movement had returned to the affrighted throng the god had gone.

IV. THE COMING OF EVIL

It came to pass that soon after these things the king fell ill and died and was gathered to his fathers; and, because he left no one to succeed him, it behoved the nobles and counsellors of the realm to choose one to reign in his stead. With one accord they prayed Osiris to accept the crown, but he would not; until at length, seeing they would make no other ruler over them, and that without a king they were fast becoming like unto sheep without a shepherd, he yielded to their entreaties.

For many years did he and his consort Isis rule the land, and he continued to instruct the people in those arts that had so greatly helped them when first he came among them. Gradually he extended his rule far beyond the confines of Egypt, subduing the people not by force of arms, but by gentle words and a knowledge of the arts of agriculture and other peaceful pursuits that hitherto had been unknown. Ofttimes on such travels he was absent many months, and Isis ruled in his stead. To the love and honour which her gentleness and kindness had inspired was added a reverence second only to that shown Osiris, by reason of her ability and wisdom in government when she was left alone.

One day there came to the gates of the palace at Thebes a stranger, accompanied by a train of armed men. Tall was he and strong, but the most ill-favoured man that the guard of the gate had ever seen. With long arms swinging loosely by his side, a huge head set on a short, thick neck, beetling brows, nose thick and squat, upper lip cut, imparting an evil sneer at all times to his face, he was a man to terrify even the brave keeper of the gate.

" Who art thou, and what seekest thou here ? " asked the soldier, when he had clanged-to the massive gates.

" Is this the palace of Osiris ? " inquired the stranger.

" It is," answered the man. " What wouldst thou have of it ? "

" Go thou and tell him that his brother Typhon hath come, and would fain yield him a kinsman's greeting," replied the giant.

" Thou his brother ! " exclaimed the guard ; and

The Kingdom of Osiris

he laughed aloud. Impossible that such a monster could be brother to their godlike king!

The stranger grew angry. "Yea, his brother," he bellowed. "Hasten with my message, or I will pull these gates about thy ears, and then spit thee on my pike." And, stretching forth a great hairy hand, he seized a bar of the gate and shook it as though to tear it from its socket.

The guard deemed it best to humour him. "I will send one with thy message," said he; and, turning, bade a comrade carry the news to the palace. To his surprise the man returned commanding that the strangers should be admitted and escorted to the presence of the king.

Osiris stood on the topmost of the entrance steps awaiting his brother. He welcomed him to the city and begged him to abide with him in the palace, where apartments were already being prepared for his use. But many a man who stood around noticed that the king's greeting lacked somewhat of its wonted cordiality; while the evil leer on Typhon's face was remarked by all.

From this time forth the peace and happiness that had marked Osiris's reign seemed to depart. In field and city smouldered a spirit of restlessness. How it came or whence no man could tell. Men were more prone to quarrel and to grumble against their lot; yet none could say wherein lay the cause of his discontent. But insensibly they often found themselves wishing for the days before the king's brother came into their midst.

Typhon took no part in the government. In truth, Osiris knew him too well to entrust any share of it to him. When not carousing with his fellows in his apartments he would set out on long hunting expeditions, from which he sometimes did not return for many months. In his absence the Thebans again dwelt in content; yet most guessed that the giant was plotting against his brother, and that his seeming love of the chase was but a cloak to hide his evil plans.

When Osiris was away Isis was so vigilant that Typhon had no opportunity to work any harm. More cautious even than the king, she never allowed the knave to leave the city without sending some trusty servant to watch and to report to her all his doings.

So the years passed by, Isis and Osiris always striving to improve the lot of their subjects and to increase their happiness; Typhon waiting and watching for a chance to seize this fair land for his own, and his hatred against his brother growing ever fiercer in his heart.

V. THE MURDER OF OSIRIS

For many days the king's brother had remained shut up in his rooms. To all inquirers he surlily replied that he wished only to be left alone; even his boon companions were excluded. These spent the time in riotous living and stirring up brawls, until the captain of the guard seized a dozen of them and kept them in

The Kingdom of Osiris 67

close confinement; whereon, though their shameless revelries were no wise checked, they were more heedful to practise them secretly.

Typhon, however, kept to himself. Sometimes he would not touch the food served up to him, and on such days the menials learnt to flee his cruel wrath. Of a sudden he sprang from his couch. "I can do it, and I will," he said.

Crossing over to a heavy wooden chest he took therefrom a long roll of cloth. This cloth was different from that worn by the Egyptians. It was softer, smoother, and in the sun shone rainbow-hued. Taking this with him the knave went forth to seek Osiris.

As chance would have it, the king was alone. "How fare you, brother?" he said kindly. "I hope your sickness has left you."

" 'Tis quite gone," replied Typhon; and you would not have known him for the Typhon of old, so gentle and bland were air and voice. "Quite gone, and I thank you for your brotherly solicitude; in token whereof I wish to make you a small gift. What think you of this?" and he proffered the roll of cloth to the king.

"It is indeed beautiful," replied Osiris. "There is not its like in this land."

"Therefore it should clothe a king," said Typhon. "If my brother will accept it, it shall be made into a robe for him, worthy of his kingly form."

"I thank you for your generosity," answered Osiris,

with no suspicion of evil. "Do you desire it, I will accept the cloth, but it shall not cause you further trouble. Leave it to the robemakers of my court. I will bid them see to it."

"That would be to deprive the robe of half its beauty," said Typhon. "I know a cunning craftsman, whose work is as superior to that of your court-followers as is this cloth to that of your weavers. Let me but take what measurements are needful, and my pleasure shall be to see it finished for you."

"So be it then, if you will," agreed the monarch; and he stood up while Typhon measured off on the cloth his length from head to heel.

"But sooth, the robe is not to cover my head also, is it?" said the king laughing.

"Ah! to be sure not," cried the rogue, in pretended confusion; and he marked off on the cloth the length from shoulder to the ground. In like manner he took other measurements, until at length he announced that they were complete.

"Ere long it shall be ready," he said. "I will take it to my craftsman at once."

When he had gained his own apartments, he summoned his followers, and in an hour they were hurrying away to the south. Toward evening they came to a marsh, on the shores of which stood a small hut.

"Wait here," said Typhon, and he strode off toward the hut, the roll of cloth under his arm. The business took long to settle, and, had anyone been near, he would have wondered both at the constant repetition of directions and yet more at the directions themselves. Carving, gilding, inlaying, are not words applied to the making of robes; yet these were the burden of the talk. Moreover, when Typhon emerged from the hut, the roll of cloth was still in his possession.

Again the party set out, riding most of the night. In two days they came to another lonely hut, and here the cloth was left with full instructions as to its disposal. Once more they took to the road, and after seventeen days came to the capital of Ethiopia.

On his arrival Typhon went straight to the royal palace and demanded admittance. Without delay he was ushered in, and forthwith conducted to the dusky queen.

"Well, hast thou been successful?" she asked.

"Not yet," replied Typhon. "They are ever on the watch. I fear the queen suspects, yea, mayhap knows somewhat of my plans."

"Not yet," repeated the other, ignoring his last remark. "Always the same story thou bringest. I thought thou wert sure of victory last time."

"Dear Aso," answered Typhon, "no one could do more than I have done. But the first step rests on guile, not on force. Afterward the more strength I can show the better."

"Well?" questioned the other briefly, as he ceased.

"I have a plan," said Typhon. "'Tis for that I am come hither. It is sure to succeed if I can lure Osiris from his watchful wife. Thou hast the troops ready to aid me?"

"My promise still holds good," replied Aso.

"Then we start back to-morrow," said Typhon, "and this time shall see me victorious."

On the following day the return journey was begun. Besides his seventy-two companions he had now a large body of soldiers in his train. On the seventh day he, with a score of his followers, rode ahead, bidding the remainder come after with all speed.

Day and night they rode, resting only for a few hours at noon and midnight. When they reached the hut where the cloth had been left, Typhon stopped, and called the man to the door.

"Hast thou finished?" he demanded.

"All is ready," replied the man. "Will my lord see the robe?"

"No, I know 'twill be well," replied the giant. "Give it, and let me be gone."

Again they hurried onward, and twice had the Sun-god made the circuit of heaven when they arrived at the hut by the marsh. As before Typhon entered alone and remained closeted with the hermit workman. Then he came to the door and called up his company.

"We will finish our journey by way of the river," he said. "Take this and put it on the boat ye will find hidden at the entrance to the marsh."

The object to which he pointed was something concealed beneath a skilfully plaited cover of papyrus.

The Kingdom of Osiris

In appearance it was like a long box—a coffin, as one remarked to his companion. But their master did not explain, and they knew better than to ask; so without more ado they carried it down to the boat. Then they pushed out of the narrow channel into mid-river, and were carried swiftly down the stream.

The following night the boat reached Thebes, and was drawn up at the steps leading to that part of the palace where Typhon dwelt. The mysterious object was lifted out, and quietly carried within.

Next morning Typhon waited upon the king, taking with him the robe he had promised. When the brothers had saluted, Typhon presented the garment.

"Will my lord be pleased to wear it?" he asked.

"Certainly, my brother," replied Osiris. "Let me put it on now."

The robe fitted perfectly, and as it hung from his shoulders, shimmering in the morning sunlight, it added dignity even to his regal figure.

"It is indeed a royal gift," he said, "and I thank thee for it. What can I give thee in return?"

"The pleasure of thy company in this robe at a banquet in my hall this night," said the crafty rogue, smiling. "So seldom is my table graced with thy presence that a visit will more than repay me for the little trouble the robe hath cost."

Now Osiris had no liking for the banquets of his brother, for he knew they were wont to develop into wild and drunken orgies, for which he felt an utter loathing. But he could not well seem churlish now; and perhaps it was not altogether his brother's fault that his instincts led him into such shameless courses, he thought generously.

When Typhon had departed Osiris sought the queen and showed her the beautiful present he had received. He told her, too, of his promise to eat with his brother that evening.

Isis looked up in alarm. "But thou saidst thou wouldst never go there again," she answered.

"After such a kindly deed, how could I refuse so small a favour?" said Osiris.

"'Tis Typhon's treachery," cried the queen in great fear. "There is some evil behind this that thou wottest not of."

"Art thou not a little unjust toward him?" asked the king gently. "He hath not been favoured in many ways as we have."

"I am sorry for him, but I am not unjust," replied the queen, her eyes full of tears. "His misshapen body is the image of a misshapen mind. He designeth evil against thee, and I pray thee go not to-night."

Now, though Osiris and Isis were in truth god and goddess, they had lived so long among men and women and had entered so completely into their thoughts, their joys and sorrows, hopes and fears, that they had become more than half human themselves, stirred by the same feelings and passions. And that day her human heart spoke loudly of impending sorrow, and

The Kingdom of Osiris 73

urged Isis to plead yet again with her husband, as she clung passionately to him.

"What ill could he do me?" said Osiris. "Moreover, in my own palace he would not dare attempt anything against my person. Yet, to calm thy fears, I promise to return ere midnight," he concluded, as he embraced her fondly.

All that evening the heart of the queen troubled her Strange and horrid shapes danced and grimaced before her, and once the air was suffused with red. She retired to her chamber and lay down on the couch, but sleep refused to kiss her eyes. Away on the other side of the great courtyard she could see the bright lights of the banqueting-hall, whence came the sounds of wild laughter and high revelry.

Meanwhile the banquet was served, a feast worthy of a king. At one end of the table sat Osiris, and at the other his brother. Dish after dish of rare meats and choicest dainties was brought, and the winecups were kept full by the watchful servitors. When at length the meal was over, Typhon, who had apparently succumbed more and more to the influence of the wine. jumped up.

"A pledge!" he shouted. "Pledge me, O king, and ye, my friends, drink to his Majesty, the mighty King of Egypt."

A shout of glee rent the air. The pledge was drunk, and Typhon spoke again.

"Much have I heard," he said, "of the cunning of

the workmen of Egypt. But, my brother, when of late I was absent travelling in distant lands, I chanced upon a wondrous box, so marvellously wrought that I declare its equal does not anywhere exist. Let me show it to you, O King."

Thereupon Typhon commanded his servants to undo the wrappings of the mysterious box that lay at the end of the hall, and to bring it forward into the light. As the papyrus rolled away, cries of amazement and delight burst from all present. There it lay, a long box of wondrously wrought metal, with strange symbols and devices worked into the lotus-lily patterns. Upon the inner surface of the lid the double crown of Egypt was picked out in precious stones.

Every one expressed his admiration for the beautiful object, and Osiris admitted that no workman known to him could have made it. The excitement increased, the babel grew louder, when suddenly Typhon, who seemed to have grown ever more reckless, shouted, " I will give the box to whomsoever it fits perfectly."

The menials had retired from the hall, and on the word the roisterers rushed toward the box. One after another climbed in, and, amid shouts of boisterous merriment, was dragged out by the rest, who each sought to claim the treasure for his own. But it was far too big for any of them.

" O King, will you not try ? " cried Typhon. " 'Twould make a fitting coffer for your robe."

The king protested, laughing at the conceit; but,

to humour the company, now frenzied with excitement, he rose from his seat and stepped to the box. He failed to see the baleful light that gleamed in the monster's eyes and the fingers trembling with eagerness as they stretched involuntarily toward the lid. As he lay down another cry of utter astonishment burst from all around. For the box fitted him as perfectly as if it had been made for him: as, in fact, it had.

Then, before he could move to get out, Typhon, with a fierce shout, crashed down the cover and slid home the bolts. Those in the plot brought nails and fastened down the lid. To make it doubly sure, molten lead was poured round the edges and the box absolutely sealed.

"Into the river with it," shouted Typhon; "and then hie ye to the frontier where our friends await us. Egypt is ours."

Stilling the tumult they passed out of the hall and down the steps to the river, into which the box was plunged. The swift-flowing waters whirled it round and round, sucking it ever toward the middle of the stream, and, as the current caught it, launched it forward. At the same instant from out the turbid depths there rushed a lurid flame that lighted up the palace and the town like day.

Typhon stood alone on the shore, his companions having already taken to the boats; and, as the light fell athwart the stream, he cried aloud in fear. Then, seizing a boat, he rowed for life in the wake of his fleeing men.

Meantime, exhausted with her anxious vigil, the queen had fallen into a fitful slumber, only to be haunted by such hideous dreams that she sought to keep awake. Again the red mist clouded her sight, and, as the last fierce shout from Typhon's hall awoke her, she saw Osiris, his face streaming with blood, his hand pointing upward. With a heart-rending cry she sprang from the couch to where the vision stood, but her arms clasped empty air. In utmost terror she waited for the coming of her lord, listening to the noises below. At length the shouts grew still, and soon there followed the sound of oars beating rapidly on the water. "Now will Osiris come," she said.

At that moment the flame leapt up from the river, and, her fears increased a thousandfold, Isis stared with tear-stained eyes upon the river scene. She caught a glimpse of Typhon springing into a boat and fleeing madly up the river before the flame died out. One by one the last faint sounds faded away in the distance, and the town was enwrapped in peace. Still Isis waited. But he for whom she waited would come no more. For Osiris, King of Egypt, was dead, the victim of a brother's hatred.

CHAPTER VII
The Quest of Isis

I. THE BEGINNING OF THE QUEST

IT was almost dawn before Isis awoke from the swoon into which she had fallen. At first she looked about her dazed and bewildered, wondering what had happened; then with a rush the events of the previous night crowded into her memory, and she fell back, overwhelmed with horror. Rousing herself with an effort, she began to make arrangements for the future. Well she knew that her lord was dead, and the hand that had sent him to his doom would quickly return to seize the crown. She feared, too, that Typhon had still more terrible designs, and soon her fears proved true.

Ten days after the murder of the king a mighty army encamped on the plain before Thebes. As evening drew in a herald approached the gates and asked to see the queen. This request Isis refused, and bade him send by the captain of the guard any message he had to deliver. Soon the soldier returned, and, making a deep obeisance, spoke.

"Typhon, King of Egypt, sendeth humble greetings

to his sister Isis. If Isis will consent to marry him, she still shall share the throne and government as heretofore. But if Isis refuse then will Typhon wage war against court and city till not one stone be left upon another, nor man nor woman live to tell the tale."

"What sayest thou, Hotep?" said Isis, when the captain ceased; for this officer was the same whom Osiris had saved from the tyranny of the king who ruled before him.

"That I would I had the vain boaster before me, O Queen," answered Hotep, "free to work my will upon him for as long as a man may count a hundred. Egypt would then be rid of its evil."

"And the other officers, what will they say?" she asked.

"What I have said, your Majesty," he answered. "Our forces are small, for the base wretch hath taken advantage of the absence of those troops that went to the land of the north; but we shall not yield the city while one man remaineth alive to defend it."

"I know thou wilt do thy best," replied the queen; "but I fear our power is too weak to withstand him. Go now, and make such arrangements as thou deemest best. For me I spurn the offer as worse than death. Whatever betide I shall soon leave Thebes. I must go and search for Osiris, my lord and thine."

"I pray you may find him, O Queen," said Hotep reverently.

The Quest of Isis

For six days the defence held out, but on the seventh a breach was made in the walls, and Typhon's black horde poured in. Men, women, and children were slaughtered until the streets ran blood, and the dead lay in heaps. Then the enemy came to the palace, where the remnant of the faithful army had gathered.

Typhon again sent in his offer to Isis, but she would not deign to reply. To wed the murderer of her husband, to accept him as king and lord! The very thought made her burn with shame. Next day his soldiers succeeded in scaling the outer wall, and Isis knew that the end was near.

She retired to her room, and, after distributing gifts to her hand-maidens and bidding them escape by the river-gate while yet there was time, commanded that she should be left alone. Taking off her outer robe, she arrayed herself in white samite. Over this she let fall her long bright hair, that shone in the sun like a radiant flame.

Stretching herself on the couch, with arms outspread, she began to chant a hymn, strange and mystical. As she sang, all around her slowly changed. The walls of the room faded away into the distance, the furniture, the very couch on which she lay, became impalpable; everything grew formless, unreal, seeming but "the baseless fabric of a dream." The clash of arms without drew nearer, but Isis heeded it not. To things of earth she was bound no more. Not for naught had she studied enchantments; not in vain had she wrested the words of power from Ra.

Dashing aside the faithful girl who sought to guard the sanctity of her queen, Typhon burst into the room. But no beautiful woman stood before him. As his foot crossed the threshold, a bird resembling a large swallow, with a crest of feathers that gleamed like burnished copper, rose from the couch, and, with a mournful cry, floated through the window and out over the river.

The quest of Isis for Osiris had begun.

II. THE STORY OF THE SATYR

Isis knew not which way to turn to find the body of her husband, but as she flew along she sometimes descended to earth in human form and inquired of those she thought might help her. For some days she learned nothing; then one day hope was born within her.

A woman of the people knelt beside the river, drawing water, and Isis approached her to ask if she had seen aught of the chest floating down the stream. The woman replied that she had not, but her husband, who was a shepherd, had heard of some such thing. Early one morning he surprised a number of strange creatures in the valley below. They had faces and bodies like men, she said, but the legs and feet of goats, and from the sides of their heads goats' horns grew. They were called Satyrs, and their ruler was named

The Quest of Isis

Pan, and the shepherds looked on them as the guardians of their flocks.

"One of the Satyrs came up to my husband," said the woman. "At first he was frightened and would have run away, for it is unlucky to meet a Satyr after sunrise. Then he noticed the sun had not yet risen, for he was in a narrow valley; so he stood still until the god came to him."

"What did the Satyr say?" queried Isis eagerly.

"He bade my husband attend carefully to his words. The night before while the Satyrs were sporting in the reeds hard by the river, a pale light came floating down the stream, and in the midst of the light a box. 'That box,' he said, 'contains the body of your king. It is going straight downstream. Remember.' Before my man could speak the Satyr had run back to his companions, and the next instant they had all vanished. But surely," added the woman, "the king could not have been in that box. He is in Thebes." And her eyes looked for support to the face of the beautiful woman beside her.

"The Satyr spake truth," said Isis. "Your king hath been cruelly done to death, and his body cast away. One who loved him seeketh him."

The sorrowful eyes filled with tears. The peasant woman fell on her face in the sand, and kissed the hem of Isis' robe. "My gracious queen," she murmured; "we who live so far away knew nothing of it. May heaven guide you in your search!"

82   Egyptian Gods and Heroes

Away went Isis, following the course of the river. She had news now, true and clear, and swiftly she sped above the water. Near the head of the delta she came to another pause. Here the river divided into two wide channels, and she knew not which to follow. To take the wrong branch would mean much loss of time, perhaps the loss of her husband's body.

In this perplexity she came upon a number of little children playing beside the river. She loved all children, and, thinking they might distract her from her sorrow for a while, she came down to earth, and, assuming her human form, drew near to them.

One of the little ones was weeping bitterly, and in another moment Isis had him in her arms. To all her questions he would answer nothing; only he gazed across the river as if seeking something. She thereupon began to question the others, when straightway the weeper began to speak.

"I want the pretty box," he said. "Which box?" asked Isis. "The pretty shining box that was in the river," he replied. "In the river? Where?" she asked quickly. There could not be two chests in the river, she thought.

"There, in the reeds," answered the boy.

"What kind of box was it?" asked the queen.

"Long and bright and shining," he answered, "with pretty flowers on it; and I touched it, but I could not lift it."

"When was it there?" she said.

"Yesterday morning," replied the child. "I went home to fetch my father to get it out of the reeds, and when we came back, it was floating away down the river."

"Poor little boy," she said. "Never mind, I will give you another box. Come here to-morrow morning, and you shall find a pretty box that you can take away yourself."

"A bright box?" asked the child eagerly, his former sorrow already forgotten in the anticipation of a new treasure. "Will it be shining, and have flowers on it?"

"Bright and beautiful as the other," answered Isis; "but smaller that you may carry it yourself. Now tell me which way this box in the river went."

"Down that stream," said the boy, pointing to one of the two big channels.

"Thank you," she said. "Now I am going to find it."

"Will you bring it back for me?" cried the boy.

"Not that one," said Isis. "I may not find it. But whether I do or not, your little box shall be waiting for you here to-morrow."

And, when the little fellow ran early next morning to the place by the river where he had met the goddess, there on the sand, shining in the rays of the rising sun like silver, lay a curiously wrought box; and in the joy of its possession the lost one was quickly forgotten.

The search was renewed, Isis expecting every hour to come up with the chest. But in the delta the river widened out and in many parts was little more than a vast marsh with papyrus growing thickly out of the water. Thus it behoved her to take the utmost care, lest she should pass it by; and many days sped away without any trace of the chest being seen.

One evening about sunset a large swallow alighted on the cross-tree of a ruined hut that stood on the shore of a marsh. The bird seemed weary, for its head drooped, and it swayed as though blown by the breeze. After some moments it looked around and spoke, as to itself.

You will have guessed that the bird was Isis, tired with the long and fruitless search. She had followed the windings of the river, exploring each papyrus clump, scanning every overhanging bush, but not a sign of the chest could she discover. She had now approached the mouth of the river, and was wondering if the box could have escaped her vigilance, or if it had been carried straight on and was now out upon the broad bosom of the sea. Many months had elapsed since the search began, and sometimes she was filled with despair.

"I will rest here in this hut for the night," she said to herself. "Perhaps to-morrow will see the end." Often had she comforted herself with the same hope, but the morrow went and the end came not.

She was about to descend from the roof of the hut, when from a grove of sycamore trees she heard the sound of shrill music, followed by peals of laughter. In a moment she was flying above the trees, in the

The Quest of Isis 85

direction of the voices, and came to a sudden stop as her eyes fell on the peculiar scene below.

At one side of a glade fringed with wild rose and jasmine, honeysuckle and trumpet-flower, a man was seated on a fallen tree, and round him were gathered a number of tiny people, chattering and laughing and clapping their hands with delight. In his hand the man held a musical instrument, made of a set of reeds of various lengths skilfully fastened together. When he put it to his lips it gave forth the most enchanting music, and the little folk at once spread out and began a stately dance. Then Isis could see that the man was not really a man at all, for he had goat's legs and on his head were two horns.

It was Pan, the most famous of all musicians, playing for his little friends the elves and fairies. As his music rang out, they advanced and retired, at first gravely and in measured step, then wheeling and turning, and finally spinning round and round in wild abandon. Faster went the music, and faster flew the tiny feet, until the dancers were an indistinct, whirling mass of colour. With a high clear note the music ceased, the blurred mass resolved itself into fairy shapes, and with shouts of happy laughter they gathered round the music-god.

"Dear Pan! Kind Pan!" they cried. "Another dance, Pan. Just one more! They are never the same as when you pipe for us."

"Not to-night," said Pan. "To-morrow if ye

will; but now I must away to the Satyrs who await my coming. To your homes, friends all, and I will pipe a measure as ye go." He took up his reed and played again as the merry throng tripped away, singing a lilting song the while.

The half-man was about to move from the tree whereon he sat, when he became aware of another figure before him, no elf this time, but of human shape.

"Thou art Pan?" queried the newcomer.

"I am, Beautiful One," he replied.

"Thou hast seen a wonderful chest floating down the river. Canst tell me whither it is gone?"

"The chest wherein lay the body of Osiris," said Pan. "Yes, I saw it. You will not find it here. It is gone."

"Gone!" cried Isis. "Gone! Shall I never see my lord again?" And all the weariness and grief and heartache of the world welled up in her cry of despair.

"Be not disheartened," said the half-man. "Though the chest is gone, mayhap it is not irrecoverable. The power of Isis is great. But hark! The fairies sing to you, and their knowledge is wide as the sea."

As he spoke, there came borne on the soft night air a low throbbing note, gentle and sweet and full of compassion. It rose and fell, as the breeze wafted the strains of the invisible choir through the glade, and Isis listened with rapt attention, her heart drinking in every word of this song.

Beautiful lady, lo! him whom thou seekest
   Not here on Nilus' dark waters thou'lt see;
If thou wouldst find him, go, leave these sad
   marshes,
Search in the heart of the tamarisk tree.

There close enwrapped by its wide-spreading
   branches
   Typhon's fell work lies concealed from the
     sight;
Cruelty shameless, dark deed of the monster,
Soon by thy love to be brought to the light.

Faint not, nor weary; thy task is nigh ended;
   Love great as thine must prevail by its might.
Then shall the lord of the world rule in glory,
   Wrong vanquished, Truth 'stablished, Darkness
     made Light.

The music ceased, yet still Isis listened. It had soothed her, and she thought she might learn yet more of her lost lord. Then, leaning forward to the Satyr, she said, "What is this I hear about a tamarisk tree and Typhon's cruelty, the defeat of wrong and the triumph of right? Knowest thou further of these things?"

"Listen, O Goddess," said Pan, "and I will tell you what I know. Many days past, the chest you seek floated down-stream and was carried far out to sea, to be tossed about by the waves until it was cast up at Byblos into the branches of a tamarisk tree."

"And shall I find it there now?" cried Isis eagerly.

"Not so," answered Pan. "The tamarisk tree grew so quickly that soon it had enfolded the box in its midst and it could not be seen. The King of Byblos, riding by when hunting, remarked the huge size of the tree-trunk, and resolved to remove it."

"Well?" said the queen impatiently, as he paused.

"Next day," continued Pan, "an army of men came with axes and ropes and cut down the tree, placed it on a waggon, and carried it off to the king's palace, where it was set up as a pillar to support the roof."

"With the chest still inside it?" asked Isis.

"Yes," replied Pan. "No one save my brothers and myself knew of its existence, and we would not speak. So there it remains, upholding the roof of the king's house."

"The thanks of Isis are thine," said the queen. "Is there anything I can do to show my gratitude?"

"The power of Isis is great," replied Pan. "I am ugly, having neither the dignity of man nor the grace of an animal. Both laugh at me and make a mock of my deformity. I pray you grant me some gift that shall make them hereafter think kindly of me."

"Thy prayer is granted," answered Isis. "Henceforth when men speak the name of Pan, it shall be in admiration of his music."

So to-day there are thousands of people who could not tell you what Pan was like, but they know that he was a god of olden times who played divinest music on a pipe of reeds.

III. THE SECRET OF THE TREE

The walls of the palace of King Melecander gleamed white in the morning sun. Not a breath stirred the air. Even the water that plashed in the marble fountain seemed to rise and fall lazily. The acacia grove looked very inviting, and a woman, tired and travel-stained, halted to rest in its welcoming shade.

Many paused to question the beautiful sad-eyed woman, but to one and all she answered nothing; only when the Queen's waiting-girls came tripping through the grove did she show any sign of interest in her surroundings. They started to see the stranger, for, save those whose business took them to the palace, no one was allowed here, nor dare they linger, however attractive the shade might be. One, a pretty maid of fourteen summers, went up to her.

"Seek you anyone here, lady?" she asked.

"Yes," answered the traveller. "The lord of all the world is here, and I come to find him."

"The king is away hunting," said the girl, for she thought the stranger spoke of her royal master.

"I said not your king," was the reply. "The stranger seeketh another stranger, long in your midst, unknown to you all, his name on every tongue." Seeing the mystified look on the girl's face, "Come here," she said, "and tell me of this place."

Like every girl the maid was willing enough to talk on that which interested her, and soon was chattering away as if she had known the lady all her life. As she knelt before her, Isis, for it was she, toyed with the girl's hair, plaiting it into a long coil that fell to the ground.

"Who are you?" asked the girl.

"The nurse of my people," was the reply.

Again the child looked puzzled. But a nurse, that at least she understood. "Can you heal anyone who is ill?" she asked.

"If I will," replied the other.

The girl remained thoughtful. Of a sudden a great bell clanged out, and she started up. "I must go now," she said. "Do you live here, or are you going away again?"

"When the tree yieldeth up the god who lieth at its heart, I go," said the woman. The girl looked wistfully at her, but could make nothing of her words and the bell clanging out once more, she hurriedly said good-bye.

The other maidens had disappeared, and, by the time she reached the royal apartments, two of them were already returning in search of her. "The Queen would speak with you," they said.

"Thou art late, Melita," said the Queen, when she entered. "Dost thou play alone that thou comest not with thy sisters? Or is it," she added, as her eye fell on the coil in which Isis had bound the girl's hair, "is it thy vanity that taketh so long to satisfy? Who did this, child?" she continued, without waiting for

The Quest of Isis

a reply, "thou couldst not alone have braided thy hair like this."

"A lady in the acacia grove did it," said the frightened Melita. "While I spoke to her she tired my hair. She saith she is a nurse, and I wondered if she could cure the prince, O Queen."

"A nurse forsooth!" cried the Queen contemptuously. "Think'st thou that where the court physicians fail, a wandering nurse-woman can succeed! But with what hath she anointed thy hair? It smelleth of primroses and violets and other fragrant flowers that love not the burning sun of Byblos. Who is this woman?"

"She said she was the nurse of her people," replied the girl. "When I asked her if she dwelt here she said, 'When the tree yieldeth up the god at its heart, I go.' What she meant I know not, O Queen. Perhaps you understand, lady."

Now Astarte, the queen, knew no more of what was meant than did the maid, but she would not say so. She stood thoughtful for a few moments; then, turning to the child, "Fetch the stranger here," she said.

Melita gladly ran back to the grove, where she found the lady gazing out over the lake as absently as when she first saw her. "The Queen desires to see you," she said. "Will you come?" She did not say the queen had commanded her presence, for in some unknown way she felt it would be an indignity to her, and, moreover, this woman might refuse to obey even the Queen herself.

"I will come," she said, after a moment's pause. "Lead on." And together they crossed the greensward to the massive pylon fronting the palace. As Isis stepped across the threshold a great trembling came upon her. She knew the treasure was at hand.

In the hall her eyes fell upon a magnificent pillar supporting the roof. It was the trunk of a single tree, straight and firm, but most wondrous were the markings on the bark. Figures of men and animals wrought amid a tracery of lotus-flowers seemed to have been graven upon it; and, high above all, on the side facing the door, was represented the crown of the kings of the North and South. On closer approach it was revealed, however, that the devices had not been carved into the bark, but were a natural growth; and this peculiarity and the beauty of the pattern had led King Melecander to cut down the tamarisk tree and bring it to his palace.

For a moment Isis stood motionless. Her face paled, and her limbs shook beneath her. At last her wanderings were o'er. Here she had found the burial-place of her lord, and soon would come reward and rest. Then, even as Melita turned round to see wherefore she lingered, she recovered herself and moved on, following the tiring-maid through the maze of rooms.

As she passed, the chatter of the waiting-women and girls ceased or fell to whispers. Was this regal figure only a nurse? Could she be a wanderer on the face of the earth ? But Isis heeded none of them, and with eyes fixed on the vision of future happiness that now rose bright before her, she proceeded to the Queen's chamber.

Astarte eyed her with wonder and somewhat of awe. This was not the sort of woman she had expected. The haughty words with which she would have greeted her died on her tongue. Suddenly a shaft of sunlight fell athwart the ruddy hair, turning it to a crown of flame. Perchance some long-forgotten memory was awakened at the sight; mayhap she guessed something of the truth. So, when she spoke, her voice was gentle and kind.

"This maid telleth me thou art a nurse," said Astarte. "Couldst nurse my child and cure him ? "

"Nurse him, yes," answered Isis. "Whether I cure him or not will depend on thee."

"Bring the prince hither," commanded the Queen, turning to Melita. "Who art thou, and whence comest thou ? " she asked. "Thou bringest with thee the fragrance and perfume of the spring flowers on my native mountains. Art of this land ? No ? "

"I came from a land far, far to the west," replied Isis. "Long I lived happily with my husband among our people. Then was he cruelly done to death, and I was driven away."

"Poor woman," said the Queen. "Thou, too, hast tasted the bitterness of sorrow."

Melita entered with a nurse bearing the prince on a

cushion. "Knowest thou what aileth him?" asked Astarte anxiously, taking the babe to Isis. "He wasteth away, and our most skilled physicians can do naught. Make him well and strong, and the King will refuse thee nothing. And the prayers of a grateful mother will alway go with thee," she added, the tears springing to her eyes.

Without a word Isis laid the babe on her arm. He moaned as in pain, and the pinched wan face was marked with suffering. Placing her finger-tips on his brow, she gazed intently at the closed eyes. They opened, and a faint smile flickered on the white lips. Next she pulled back his silken robe, drew her cool hand down the thin body, and finally put her finger in his mouth, at which for some minutes he sucked vigorously. Then she handed him back to his mother. "Your child will be well," she said simply.

In three more days the little boy was running about in all the wanton joy of childhood; and Isis had been installed as mistress of the royal nursery.

IV. THE REVELATION OF THE GODDESS

Day by day the royal boy grew stronger and handsomer, and his quickness and intelligence were remarked by all. He had been healed when doctors had failed; and seemingly the mysterious nurse had power also to improve his mind as well as his body. By day he was with other nurses of the palace; but at night, at Isis' request, he slept in her room, where none other was allowed to attend him.

So for many days all went well. Then began rumours of strange doings in the newcomer's room during the dark watches of the night. Unwonted sounds were heard behind the heavy doors, sounds of baby laughter mingled with the crackling of flames; bright lights were burning when all should have been asleep; and the music of a woman's beautiful voice, clear and soft as a distant evening bell, floated on the still night air. Yet when the ancient dame, aforetime charged with the prince's safety, knocked at the chamber door, the lights went out, the music ceased; and, on entering the room, child and nurse were both found fast asleep.

Twice had fate thus cheated her, and she resolved that the Queen must learn of these proceedings. A long tale she poured out, in fear and anger. "I am not the only one, O Queen, to hear and see things," she said. "All your waiting-women have witnessed that I have seen. Nay, more; the guard in the hall says that, ever since the strange woman arrived, a swallow comes from her room every night about the middle watch and flies round the big carved pillar in the hall, uttering mournful cries. Once he started to drive the bird away, when he found he could not move, whilst it looked at him with eyes full of sorrow, the eyes, he says, of the stranger."

"Idle tales," said the Queen. "I will prove for myself the folly of your words."

That night she concealed herself in the sleeping-room of Isis. She felt it ill accorded with her queenly dignity thus to spy upon the woman who was at once her guest and her benefactor; but the story of the nurse had disquieted her, and her mother-love sought to shield her child against all harm. She watched Isis come into the room, bend over and kiss the sleeping child, and then retire to her own couch.

Hour after hour passed by, and nothing happened. The Queen began to think she was more foolish than her attendants in that she had given credence to their stories. It was very uncomfortable, too, cramped up in the narrow closet, with no chance of escape before morning. The wind sighed and moaned, sometimes rising to an angry scream, and distant mutterings foretold a coming storm. Verily it would have been much wiser, thought the Queen, to have gone quietly to bed, instead of listening to old women's tales of witchcraft, and demeaning herself in the eyes of her own household, as well as risking offence to the woman to whom she was so deeply beholden.

Suddenly every nerve in her body tingled with amaze and expectation. All the torches in the room had burst into flame, and, peering out from her hiding-place, Astarte perceived Isis standing in the middle of the room, the babe cradled on her arm. Her long hair was loose, shrouding herself and child. But what was this? From her finger-tips, from every strand of hair, trickled streams of fire; her face was lighted up like the sun at noonday, and her eyes gleamed like stars. The child laughed and cooed and screamed with delight,

The Quest of Isis

the flames blazed and crackled while she bathed the naked child in their livid glow; and mingling with the sounds came the rich low voice of Isis, chanting mysterious words in a tongue she did not understand.

For an interval while one might count a hundred, mayhap, the Queen remained spellbound; then with a shriek of utmost fear she sprang forth from her place of concealment. But ere she could take three paces forward the chamber was in darkness, save for the tiny torch that remained alight throughout the night, and Isis stood calmly in the centre of the room, the babe sleeping in her arms.

Aghast at the miraculous change, Astarte could only stare at the stranger woman, whose eyes rested on her, piercing her through and through.

"Who art thou?" she said at length, her voice hoarse with fear.

A flash of lightning illuminated the room, playing for some moments about the nurse's head before passing away and leaving them in a denser gloom.

"Unhappy woman!" said Isis. "Womanlike, thou didst fear for thy child, and thy love hath lost him immortality. This night I would have purged him from all that is mortal and endowed him as one of the gods. Thy rash interference hath broken the spell, and never now can I make him other than he is. Take him. Immortality cannot be his: old age and death must come to him as to others."

"Who art thou?" whispered Astarte again.

Flash after flash of brilliant light made the room brighter than day, the long tongues of flame flickering and dancing round the mysterious figure, and adding to the Queen's terrors a thousandfold. But that was not all. As she gazed, head forward, face white, and eyes starting from their sockets in the extremity of fear and dread, a transformation came over the woman before her. The coruscations of vivid light gathering together descended upon her head in a ball of golden fire, from which issued bright-eyed serpents with darting heads and quivering tongues, like those adorning the Egyptian crown; while Isis' flowing hair changed to wings of glistening red and blue and gold. Her face was kindly and gentle as ever, but wrapped now in the calm dignity that belongs to the gods in Aalu.

Chained to the spot, Astarte stared at the awful sight. Next moment, with a terrific crash that shook the palace to its foundations, the storm broke; and, with a shuddering wail of unutterable misery, she clasped the infant to her heart and fled from the room.

V. THE MOVING OF THE CHEST

Isis sat in the low window, gazing out over the row of acacias to the line of sand that bordered the sea. The storm of the previous night had long ago spent itself, but away to north and west the clouds were still banked up in dark and threatening masses; in the east the sun gleamed fitfully through the cloud-belt.

The Quest of Isis

The grove was strewn with wreckage and drift of the storm, and the bright-hued flowers lay whipped and torn and bedrabbled in mud. But Isis saw none of these. Her thoughts were fixed on greater things, for was not her search to end to-day? She knew the King would send a messenger to her, and she waited patiently, thinking of the happy days to come.

Meleeander was not in good humour. He had returned from his hunting to be annoyed by foolish tales about the new nurse, and in the middle of the night his rest had been disturbed by an urgent message that the Queen was beside herself with fear and called for his presence. When he reached her bedside she could at first only babble incoherently of nurse and lightning, golden wings and shining serpents, goddesses and crowns of fire, and much more that he could in no wise understand; and only after long questioning did he gather that the nurse who had so successfully tended the young Prince was in the Queen's opinion a goddess, and must be propitiated and then sent on her way.

Now had Meleeander been asked to entertain some neighbouring prince he would have done it nobly and enjoyed it too. Crocodile and hippopotamus hunting would provide sport enough during the day, and the richness of his feasts and banquets was known to all. But to get rid of a goddess-guest was a problem with which he had heretofore not met.

But it had to be faced, and, after pacing the chamber for some time, he beat sharply upon the brazen gong.

"Fetch the girl Melita," he said to the attendant who answered the summons. "I will see this stranger lady if she will admit me," he said to himself. "Haply something will transpire to show me how I should act." So when Melita came from the Queen's chamber, where she had been through this eventful night, he bade her ask Isis if she would receive him.

Wondering what these unwonted happenings might portend, the maid knocked timidly at the door of Isis' room. In answer to the command from within she entered and, curtseying humbly, advanced to the window-seat.

"The King would know if he can see you," she said, when at length words came to her.

"Yes," said Isis quietly. "Tell the King I will receive him here."

When the King entered he crossed the room and, taking the outstretched hand, knelt and kissed it. Thus did he pay homage to the goddess who was his guest.

"The Queen is not well," he began slowly; "the happenings of the night have tried her sorely. But she begs me thank you for the care you have bestowed upon the Prince our son; and no words can express my own gratitude for the favour you have shown in coming to us. Who you are I know not, but before you depart I pray you say if there be aught in which I can serve you."

"Melecander," answered she, touched by the gentle

tone and quiet dignity of the King's simple words, "Melecander, thou knowest much that thou wilt not say. For thine ease I will tell thee that the Queen will soon be well. As for thy son, his name and prowess shall in days to come be noised abroad through all the land of Byblos. For me the hour of my departure is nigh, and, ere I go, I ask a boon of thee."

"Thy wishes even now are granted," said the King.

"The pillar that stands in the great hall," said Isis, "I ask it of thee."

Melecander was not prepared for this demand. The pillar had cost him dear, in labour and treasure, to set in place, but not for that did he hesitate. The column was unique, and from far and near men came to admire the curious device that had grown in the bark. His hesitation, however, was but momentary. He had pledged his word, and, had Isis asked for the palace and all within, he would not have refused her.

"It shall be removed at once," he answered.

"You value it for that which is without," said Isis. "I seek it for that which is within. Thus may we both be satisfied."

All that day artificers were busy taking down the pillar of the tree, and next morning Isis, in the presence of the King and Queen, came into the hall to take possession. But when they would have carried it to the boat which she had asked should be in readiness for her, she bade them stay; and, taking a long knife, she drew it four times down the trunk where it lay. The outer part fell away, and there, in the heart of the tree, lay the most wondrous piece of workmanship that eye had ever beheld. It was the chest of Typhon.

For a moment her emotion overcame her, and the scene swam before her eyes. Conquering her weakness, she took a great length of pure white linen, spread it out, and laid thereon the fragments of bark. Having poured perfumed oil upon them, uttering as she did so strange and mystic words, she turned to the King.

"These sacred relics have enshrined the body of a god," she said. "Keep them with all reverence. Thus shall thy treasure be preserved to thee, and whilst thou and thy people do honour to them your land shall have the favour of the gods. Hear and remember."

Later in the day a solemn procession was formed, and the sacred tree was brought to the great temple of the city. By the King's orders, it was carefully pieced together as it had been in life, and set up above the altar of their god, where it abode for many hundreds of years, an object of reverence and awe for the miracles that it wrought.

Meantime twelve stalwart bearers had raised the metal chest and borne it to the boat. The King and Queen and all the Court had followed to the waterside to attend on the goddess as she bade the land farewell, and a great multitude of the humbler folk had gathered on the shore. The boat was draped in cloth of purple and gold, and the great sail was of black silk. Gently and with utmost reverence the chest was lowered to its place, and when all was ready Isis turned to the Queen, who led the Prince by the hand. Taking him in her arms, she passed her hand over his brow, and then kissed him long and passionately. " I loved him too," she said simply, as she gave him back to his mother.

Then she stepped into the boat and stood at the foot of the chest. The sail was run out, the chains were cast off, and, guided by invisible hands, the royal vessel dropped down the stream. The quest of Isis had ended.

CHAPTER VIII

The Persecution by Typhon

I. THE AWAKENING OF OSIRIS

UP the dark stream went the boat, amid the rustling reeds and under overhanging sycamore and lebbek trees, whose arms stretched gaunt and grim above the waters, Isis standing meantime in the stern, with eyes fixed on the chest before her. The sail's black shadow fell athwart the stream, and the dark pall gleamed dull beneath the heavy clouds. Not a living thing was to be seen; man and beast and bird had left these dreary wastes, and loneliness and death reigned there.

At about the going down of the sun the royal barge came to a reach of the river where the bank sloped away in a long sandy beach. Here for the first time Isis looked up, and, with a touch of her hand, guided the ship into a little creek thickly fringed with high-grown reeds. She stepped out and looked around; nothing here but sand and reeds and water and sky, and a few tall palms looming up a hundred yards away.

Returning to the boat, she examined the chest carefully. The long immersion in the water had rotted the wood and rusted the fastenings. With a sharp tool she quickly dug out some of the wood round the lid, and inserted in the hole the handle of an oar. As she pressed upon it, one after another the fastenings snapped, and the heavy lid swung back.

What had she expected to find within the chest? Did she know the truth? Doubtless she did. But as her eyes fell on the well-loved form and features of Osiris, as perfect and unchanged as when she last parted from him, she could not withhold a deep sigh nor check the tears that coursed down her cheeks: it was the triumph of the woman over the goddess.

For long she gazed upon him, thoughts of the happy days of old filling her mind. Never again could she listen to his loved voice nor walk with him in the cool of the evening when work was done and they were for a while alone together. Never? Perhaps not in the courts of Thebes: but, never! Not yet should that word be said.

Quickly stooping, she raised him tenderly in her arms and bore him to the strand. Next she removed her outer robe, and loosed her flowing hair that covered her with a garment of bright red gold as the rays of the westering sun fell upon it. Three times she bowed in adoration to the sun-god Ra, and then lay down, with arms outstretched and face toward the west, beside the body of the dead King.

A low song of mourning stirred the evening air. Gently it rose and fell, now swelling out into wildest passion, now dying away in infinite sorrow. There followed utter silence; then the voice of Isis chanting the fateful words of magic that she had learnt in the days of long ago.

As she sang her eyes slowly closed, and once again did peace steal o'er the scene. Not a breath stirred her body, not a feature moved. The whispering in the reeds died away, and the rustling leaves were still. To outward seeming Isis was dead like the King by her side, and nature had died in sympathy.

But what is this? From her side there rises another figure, borne on gossamer wings, that flits above the prostrate forms, and finally comes to rest beside Osiris. Is it the Queen? Surely those are the lineaments of Isis, that her graceful form! But no! The face is that of Isis, transformed with a grandeur and majesty that the earthly form never knew; the body is that of the Queen, etherealized and pure. It is the triumph of the goddess over the woman.

Her eyes bent upon the form on the sand. Such pity, such love filled them as human eyes could never show. A look of power and great resolve crossed the face, and the goddess, rising on her wings, hung above Osiris. The soft hum of her voice, as she uttered the words of enchantment, sounded like the murmur of a far distant sea, the gentle beat of her wings as the sighing of the spirits of night.

Suddenly she looks up. The Sun-god in his boat **rests** atop of yonder hill, a glorious disc of gold. The

The Persecution by Typhon 107

supreme moment has come. Now must she put to the test the secret knowledge aforetime gained from Ra. Others has she cured by enchantment, but never has she brought one back to earth from beyond the grave. One mistake now, one error of speech, one fault in sound or tone as the awful enchantment is uttered, and all the pain, the heartache, and the weariness of the past months shall have availed her naught.

But not for an instant does the goddess hesitate. No quiver in the voice, no pallor of the cheek marks the immensity of the issue of the next moment. With hands uplifted, and eyes reflecting in their depths the flaming orb in the west, at the very instant he sinks behind the hill-top to enter the valley of Amentet, she cries aloud the hidden name of Ra, the name that Isis alone of gods and men has learned, the potent name that rules the universe.

And now a miracle happens. The Boat of Millions of Years that has sunk behind the hill appears again on the summit, and in it can be seen the Sun-god Ra himself, standing, his face turned toward the group upon the sand. A livid flame overspreads the heavens and bathes the earth in blood. Then, with a crash like the crash of doom, the Boat and its dread occupant have vanished, and blackness, utter and profound, enwraps the world.

When the stars came out, and the crescent moon cast her silvery beams across the river, the goddess had gone; but two figures gently breathing, side by side upon the strand, told of the victory that love had won over evil.

II. THE SECOND MURDER OF OSIRIS

The next two years were years of great joy to the exiled King and Queen. A little hut of branches and reeds made their home; the river provided wealth of fish and wildfowl for food; and a plot of ground beyond the trees, on which were still a few stalks of corn, was tilled by Osiris to yield a prolific harvest. And when the baby Horus was born, their cup of happiness was full to overflowing.

In the evening they would sit without the hut, Osiris playing on his reed pipe while Isis crooned a lullaby over the babe in her lap; or, again, they would go for long sails on the river, wafted by the evening breeze that breathed of peace. At other times they talked softly of the future, of the wisdom of making an attack upon Typhon to wrest from him their own, watching the while the boy Horus kicking and rolling on the sand.

Verily it was a happy life, a life of joyful rest. The stress and storm of the years in Thebes was past; yet they sometimes longed to be there again. Not for themselves, oh no! But because they loved the land and its people, who were now groaning under the sway of the usurping tyrant. For by the aid of his Ethiopian allies Typhon had made himself master of the country, and ruled his subjects with a rod of iron, yea, chastised them with whips and scorpions. Hated of all was he, but his grip upon the land was too tight to permit an attempt to throw off his yoke.

Ofttimes did Isis and Osiris speak of these things, their hearts bleeding for the wrongs of their people, and many were the plans they formed for their deliverance. But seldom were these projects to be executed by their own hand; almost invariably they centred round the merry boy playing by the stream. When he had come to man's estate, then would be the hour of vengeance.

So the days slipped on into months and the months into years, and the child grew up lusty and strong and beauteous of form. Sometimes he would take one of the spears that his father had wrought for him, and catch the fish that swam in the river; or he would craftily set up a net to trap the quail and wild-duck that frequented the marge. His father taught him, too, young though he was, the use of club and spear; and it was his delight to show his mother how skilfully he could wield them, whirling the club around his head till it seemed a flashing wheel of light, and hurling the spear straight and true to its mark.

But one drop of bitterness lingered in the woman's cup of happiness. Sometimes Osiris would go off on long hunting expeditions, saying it behoved him to find fresh diet. At these times he would be absent for two or three days, and Isis lived in a fever of anxiety until she heard his cheery call across the marsh. Then she would snatch up the boy in her arms and hurry forth to welcome the wanderer, tears of relief and gladness filling her eyes.

Once he failed to return on the third evening, the longest time he had ever been away. The full moon rose, and Isis walked down to the river and along the bank, but no sign of Osiris could she see. Visions of his dead form rose before her eyes, of an iron-bound chest in which it was sealed, of that terrible night long ago when ruin and desolation stood before her. Distractedly she paced back and forth, praying the livelong night that Osiris might not be taken from her again. Just as day dawned a shout from the trees sent her flying across the waste, to be enfolded next moment in her husband's arms. He had been hunting a gazelle, and had followed it farther than he purposed; yet, knowing how anxious Isis would be, he had hurried back, travelling all night in the bright moonlight. Hereafter Osiris was careful not to be absent for more than one day at a time, and the heart of Isis was gladdened thereby.

But some months later it came to pass that he was away for two days and did not return. The third day likewise passed without him. The long, long night wore away, but no welcome shout greeted the sorrow-stricken wife. Four days, five days, six days dragged by, and no Osiris came. Then Isis knew that never would she see him more. His enemies had taken him again; and for her the sun had ceased to shine.

The Persecution by Typhon 111

She sat down in the hut, gazing with unseeing eyes across the waste of sand and water. Hour after hour passed by, and no movement betrayed that the lonely figure was alive. The little Horus came to her, and, after vainly trying to attract her attention, cried himself to sleep in her lap. To worldly things Isis was dead; and she lived only in the past.

The Boat of Millions of Years had almost completed its daily journey when, with a shuddering sigh, Isis awoke. She went down to the creek where the boat in which she had come from Byblos was kept, thinking to see if it was all in good condition, and with some vague idea of starting out in it to find the lost one. It lay close-hidden amid the reeds, and almost had she stepped into it when she saw that it had an occupant. She moved back with a little cry, that rose next moment to a shriek of terror.

"I startled thee, fair sister," said the one in the boat; and, as he looked up, he revealed the repulsive features and misshapen body of Typhon.

"I startled thee," he repeated. "Believe me, 'twas not my wish to do so, for I was coming to see thee as soon as the boat was ready. I would take thee on a journey."

Isis stared aghast at him, answering never a word. The deceit and cruelty of this monster rushed to her memory, and now she knew what had befallen her husband.

"Methinks thou art not overjoyed to see me," said

the evil one, when she did not speak. "In sooth, it is not friendly to greet me thus."

His mocking words brought Isis to herself. Calmly she walked up to him, looking him straight in the face. "Thou hast killed him?" she said.

Typhon quailed before that proud glance, but, despite himself, he felt compelled to answer.

"Yea, I killed him," he replied defiantly, yet full of fear withal.

"Wicked and cruel monster," said Isis then, "couldst thou not leave us alone here? When all the country was thine, didst thou begrudge us our happiness in this solitude? Was there still more for which thy malignant heart craved?"

"Yea," said Typhon, "it craved for thee. I would marry thee and make thee Queen again. Wilt thou accept the crown I offer?"

"Where is Osiris?" asked Isis, ignoring his words.

"Where thou shalt never find him," replied the archfiend savagely. "Not again shalt thou restore the dead to life by spells and enchantments. I surprised him as he hunted, and I slew him; and, to make sure that my end should not again be frustrated, I dismembered him and scattered the parts throughout the length of Egypt. Doth that suffice thee?"

Isis shrank not at the brutal recital, though her soul felt sick within her. Casting upon him a look of contempt, she spake. "Coward and traitor," she said, "soon shall come the day of reckoning, and in that

The Persecution by Typhon

day shall thy measure be pressed down and running over." Then turning away, she moved toward the hut.

"Stay," roared Typhon, laying a detaining hand on her arm. "Thou shalt not go from me thus. I have offered thee a throne, and thou shalt answer me."

The eyes of the goddess blazed upon him so furiously that his hand fell to his side. "Touch me again," she said, and her voice quivered with anger, "and thou shalt learn somewhat of the power of Isis. As for thee and thy thrones, I spurn them as the vermin beneath my feet."

Typhon gnashed his teeth in fury. "I, too, am a god," he cried. "Thy magic arts will not avail with me. To-morrow, whether it like thee or not, thou shalt go with me, and I will place thee where thou wilt be in safe ward. Mayhap thy proud heart will soften in time," and he laughed meaningly.

The next day, escorted by half a hundred of his choice companions, they set off up the stream, rowing hard all day until at eventide they came to a grim fortress. Here they disembarked, and Typhon led Isis and her son within the gates, that clanged to after them with a hollow sound. "The emptiness of the tomb," thought Isis.

In the hall they were met by an ancient servitor and his wife, to whose charge they were confided. Typhon gave precise commands that they were to be treated with all honour and respect, but on no account to be

H

allowed out of sight, night or day. Then, with a mocking smile to Isis, but never a word, he returned to his friends.

III. THE ESCAPE OF ISIS

Many days had Isis and Horus been shut up in the prison, and no deliverance came nigh. At first they had been visited daily by Typhon, who sought to obtain his ends by fair promises of freedom and future power; but Isis being deaf to promises and threats alike, even these visits ceased. Albeit she was thus relieved of this source of annoyance, her heart greatly misgave her; for she knew her persecutor had not abandoned his designs; his absence but betokened that he was plotting more wickedness against her.

Many a time and oft did she call on Ra to send her help, but her prayers remained unanswered. Her only visitor was the janitor who brought her food, or his wife who occasionally would come to see whether her services were needed. Her gentle disposition and kindness won their hearts, and, had it lain in their power, her keepers would readily have connived at her escape. But, had they dared, they could do nothing; for Typhon, or Set, as he was called here, had magic power too, and had enchanted them and the prison so that they knew not the way in or out.

One evening as Isis was playing with her child before the hour of sleep, a tall, grave-faced stranger suddenly appeared before her. Thinking it was one of her

The Persecution by Typhon

enemy's minions, she caught the boy and, pushing him behind her, confronted the intruder.

"Who art thou," she said haughtily, "and what seekest thou here?"

"Be not alarmed, Isis," said the stranger; "I come to aid thee, not to harm. Had I come as I am wont to appear in heaven, thou wouldst have known me. I am Thoth, sent hither by Ra to help thee escape from the hand of the tyrant and to aid in the restoration of Osiris."

Now Thoth was the wisest of all the gods; he held the keys of knowledge, and against him none might prevail. So Isis was content.

At the mention of her husband's name she would have poured out a flood of questions, but the god held up a protesting hand.

"This is no time for speech," he said. "If thou wouldst save thy life and the life of Osiris's son, prepare to follow me. Yet for thy soul's peace I will add that the day shall come when thou shalt find the body of Osiris, who, restored to life, shall rule over a kingdom greater than thou hast ever dreamed of."

This, as you already know, came to pass, for Osiris became judge of the realms of the dead; but Isis, understanding not the hidden meaning of the words, heard the god with amaze, not thinking of what kingdom greater than Egypt he spake. Yet she was gladdened and comforted at the knowledge vouchsafed her, for would she not one day meet her lord and husband

and with him be happy? She picked up her babe, therefore, and followed Thoth.

Along many a winding way they went, past doors and gates that opened at the god's potent touch, down darksome passages that shone with a mystic light as they threaded them, until at last they emerged on the open plain.

"Here I leave you," said Thoth. "I commit you both to the care of my servants and the servants of the mighty Ra. Follow them until thou comest to a certain city far away to the south that they will tell thee of, and there abide. Fare ye well." And before Isis could thank him Thoth had vanished, and the two were alone.

Where were the servants he had spoken of? She looked around, but none was in sight. Perhaps they would be long in coming, and meantime Typhon's menials might discover her escape. Should she stay where she was or hide in the papyrus until the men of Ra arrived?

"When the lady Isis is ready we will set forth," said a voice which seemed to come from under her feet.

Isis looked down, and there perceived an enormous scorpion, then another, and another, and another, until she had counted seven. Were these the servants of Thoth? Another woman would have sprung away in terror from the deadly creatures, but Isis knew that God uses the most unlikely means as his instruments.

The Persecution by Typhon

"Why are ye gathered here?" she said.

"I am Tefen," said the biggest of the scorpions. "I come to follow the lady Isis and her son Horus, and to protect them from harm."

"I am Befen," said the one next him, "and go with my brother Tefen to watch from behind."

"I am Mestet," said a third, "and will walk on the right hand of the lady Isis."

"I am Mestetef," said the fourth, "and will keep watch and ward on her left."

"We are Petet, Thetet, and Maatet," cried the other three, "and are sent by Ra to lead the lady Isis to the city of the south."

"It is well," said Isis, when they had all spoken. "Let your faces be turned to the ground that ye may show me the way."

Thus did they fare forth. For many days Isis journeyed, the sun beating fiercely down upon her, and the sand glaring until her eyes ached. Always she was oppressed, too, with the thought that Typhon would discover her flight and set out in pursuit. She would have urged her guides to hasten, impatient at the delays occasioned by the needful stops for rest; but they, directed by the divine power, never varied their pace. They knew that all was under Ra's direction and must be well.

At length they reached a city called Teb, and the scorpions informed Isis that here for the present she must abide.

IV. THE RESTORATION OF THE FEN-WOMAN'S CHILD

On arriving at Teb, Isis went to the house of the women of the overlord of that district, and asked for shelter. The chief woman, however, was angry with her because of the scorpions that were her companions, and not only refused her admittance, but forbade any of the other women to take her in. Isis was thus compelled to seek other refuge, and returned to the road that led past the marsh, where she sat down to rest.

As she leaned wearily against the trunk of a tree, a woman of the fens came by.

"You look tired, lady," said she; for, like every one else, she easily recognised the superiority of the exiled Queen. "My house is poor, and I have little to offer; but such as it is I freely give it to you. Come with me. I will carry the boy." And without waiting for a reply she picked up the child and walked toward a reed-made hut on the edge of the marsh.

There she quickly set before Isis a bowl of milk, some bread, and fruit, and while the goddess ate, the fen-woman fed Horus from another dish of milk.

By skilful questioning she discovered the treatment that Isis had received at the hands of the overlord's wife. "Verily she is a hard woman," said she, "cold and selfish. She thinks only of her own, and will help none if she can avoid it. May Ra be more merciful to her!"

The Persecution by Typhon

When it came to the ears of the overlord's wife that this woman had befriended the traveller whom she had driven out, she came down in great wrath to the hut by the marsh.

"How darest thou show favour to one whom I have frowned upon?" she cried. "Were my lord here I would have thee whipped for thy temerity."

"The lady was weary," said the poor woman humbly. "I did but give her to eat and drink and offer her my house wherein to rest a space. Could I do less?"

"Couldst thou do less!" cried the other in a fury. "Thou darest ask me if thou couldst do less! Did not I refuse her admittance because of her evil companions, and wouldst thou censure me by showing her kindness? Leave this house at once. If thou art here when my lord the governor returns on the morrow, thou shalt be flogged and put in irons."

As soon as she had gone the fen-woman burst into tears. "All I have ever loved is bound up with this house," she sobbed; "and now must I leave it. Ah, she is a cruel, cruel woman!"

"Is her husband also cruel?" asked Isis.

"No," replied the woman, "but he fears her bitter tongue and does what she commands him to do; and, would he listen to my prayers, she will not let him."

"Weep no more," said Isis. "Thou knowest not who I am, but I can help thee, and thou shalt not leave thy home."

Meanwhile the scorpions, which had marked the insult offered to their charge, held converse together as to how they might best avenge it. At length they all came to Tefen, and emptied the poison of their tails upon his tail, and thus, charged with a sevenfold measure of poison, he entered under the door of the overlord's house. Once inside, he crawled along beneath the matting that covered the floor until he came to the cot wherein lay the woman's infant son, and stung him.

The child's cries speedily brought his mother and a host of servants to see what was amiss, but he was beyond all human help. The poison, sevenfold strong, was too deadly for any remedies they knew, and in a brief space he was no more. To add to the disaster, one of the women in her excitement overturned a live brazier, and, the dry rushes catching fire, the house was soon ablaze.

While the men-servants were labouring to overcome the flames, the distraught mother went about the city uttering cries of lamentation. But none came to her call; her selfishness and hardness of heart had estranged the people from her, and in her grief she was alone. Yet there was one who felt for her. The stranger whom she had turned from her door had a son, and her mother's heart was filled with compassion for the stricken woman and for the child that had suffered through no fault of his own. As the woman passed by she called to her.

The Persecution by Typhon

"Come to me," she said, "for my speech hath in it the power to protect, and it possesseth life. I can drive out the evil from thy son by one of my utterances which my father taught me. If thou wilt, bring him hither and I will heal the boy."

At first the woman was loth to accept a favour from one whom she had so shamefully treated, and went on her way. But as none other could help her, she was at length fain to test the power of the despised stranger. So she brought the child and laid him down before her.

Then Isis placed her hands upon the dead child and spake. "O poison of Tefen," she cried, "come forth, and appear on the ground; come not in, approach not! O poison of Befen, come forth! For I am Isis the goddess, and I am she of words of power, and I know how to work with words of power, and most mighty are my words. O all ye reptiles which sting, hearken unto me, and fall down on the ground! O poison of Mestet, come not hither! O poison of Mestetef, rise not up! O poison of Petet and Thetet, enter not here! O poison of Maatet, fall down!"

Then followed the magical words that she had learned from Thoth, and that no one knew save her alone. And the shadows lengthened, and the wind fell to a gentle whisper in the reeds, and yet the child stirred not. As the sun-disk touched the distant hill-tops Isis arose, and stretching out her arms she cried, "The child liveth and the poison dieth! The sun liveth and all evil dieth!"

The waiting women looked down, and, true enough, the boy was gently breathing. "Take him," said Isis, as she turned into the hut. At the selfsame hour the men at the house overcame the flames and saved it from utter destruction, the gods having accepted the prayers of Isis on the woman's behalf.

In the dark of the night there came a gentle knock at the door of the hut, and, when the fen-woman opened it, the overlord's wife walked in. Going straight up to Isis she sat down at her feet.

"This morn I closed my door upon you," she said, very humbly. "I feared your scorpions, and I was angered that you brought them where my child was, so I turned you away. I have been punished, and I come to crave your pardon for my harshness. Will you forgive me?"

"I have naught to forgive thee," was the reply. "Thou didst act as thou deemedst best, and 'twas love for thy boy and not ill-will that prompted thee. Strive to be more thoughtful and generous hereafter, and know that love and gentleness avail more than bitterness and malice."

"Is there aught in which I can help you now," asked the other; "aught to atone for my unkindness?"

"There is one thing," said Isis. "This woman who liveth here thou hast threatened to drive from her home, the home to which her heart is given. Take back thy hasty words, and, further, as a token of thy sincerity, give the house to her as a possession so long as she shall live. To-morrow proclaim abroad the gift that all may know of thy goodness and bounty."

At first the overlord's wife was taken aback with the boldness of the request. She had been willing and even anxious to make amends to one so powerful as the stranger who had restored her son to life; but to show favour to the fen-woman, to eat her words of the morning, was more than she had counted upon. Yet, she reflected, none but themselves would be the wiser; they had been alone when she had uttered her menaces earlier in the day, and she thought she saw a way to keep the woman's tongue silent.

"If she will forget what happened this morning," she said, "and keep silence on what I spoke in my haste, I on my part will think no ill of her, but feel grateful to her for having befriended you. And to-morrow what you ask shall be done, and this house given to her and hers for ever."

"So be it," replied Isis. "The fen-woman shall remember thy words no more, but shall always speak well of thee."

With this assurance the ruler's wife returned to her house, while the woman of the fens fell on her knees and poured out a flood of thanks to the lady of mysteries.

V. THE DEATH OF HORUS

After these things it came to pass that Isis resolved to depart from Teb; the tale of her doings was noised abroad in the land, and mayhap she thought that news of her presence among them would come to the ears of Set. So she called the scorpions, and when they were all assembled she said, "Turn your faces down to the ground, and find me straightway a road to the swamps and to the hidden places in Khebet." Whereupon the scorpions turned their faces to the north and the Delta, and again the procession set out.

The land of Khebet of which Isis spoke was an enchanted isle that floated on the Nile's broad bosom, near to the town of Busiris. He who knew the secret could make this island move away from its foundations and float about the stream at will. But the secret was known to few, only Isis and her sister Nephthys, and another their friend who lived on the island, being aware of its magic properties and how to use them.

Thither, then, Isis went. The way was long and arduous, but, guided by her faithful allies, she pressed on till she came to the land of Am. There the people hailed her as a goddess, and, yielding to their entreaties, she promised to dwell awhile among them. Being near to Khebet, and needing no longer the friendly services of the scorpions, she thanked them and gave them leave to depart.

Now followed a life of restful happiness. No cruel enemy to harass her, no haunting fear that her baby boy might be snatched away by her grim foe; for him she had protected by spells and magic words culled from ancient lore, and now he was safe from Set and

The Persecution by Typhon

all his minions. The roses of life again began to bloom, and in watching her son grow up toward manhood she somewhat forgot the sorrows of the past.

Daily she went out to win food and raiment for herself and child, whom she left meanwhile with kind friends. They would fain have supplied all her needs from their own store, and felt honoured in the acceptance of their gifts; but Isis would have none of such. She would not be a burden to them; and, moreover, by going about among the people she could better glean news of her enemy.

What joy it was to come home in the cool of the day and find Horus running down the dusty path to meet her! How she laughed to see his childish efforts to use the spear and club and bow, and called him her new Osiris, her avenger! And with what a wealth of mother-love she hugged him to her heart when alone at night, and crooned her lullabies over his slumbering form! He was her all. For him and the work he had to do she lived and moved and had her being.

But with all her care she had neglected one thing, and suddenly the roses withered beneath the icy touch of death, and earth was bare and void. Once evening when she came home Horus failed to run to meet her as was his wont, and, struck with a sudden chill foreboding, she hurried forward to the house. There, stretched out on the floor, his body swollen and shapeless, his face livid, and his limbs all tense and rigid, the curly-headed boy lay—dead. She had protected him against

Set and all men, but she had overlooked the most dangerous reptile in the land; and in her absence he had been stung by a scorpion, and was now no more.

Resenting the silent reproof she had expressed at their conduct by healing the child of the woman of Teb, one of the scorpions lent her by Thoth had gone to Typhon and told him where the fugitives lay hid. But the evil one could not touch them now; the charms of Isis proved too strong for him. Wherefore he took the scorpion and by sorcery fortified its poison against the power of Isis, and bade it then return to Am and sting the boy, knowing that by his death he would hurt the mother most.

The dwellers in the swamps came round about her, and the fen-men drew near, and they seated themselves on the ground and wept at the greatness of her misery. Yet no one opened his mouth to speak to her; words would have seemed sacrilege at such a time, and they sat around in silent sorrow. The women, too, assembled and mourned with her; and one of them, the wife of a great ruler of the district, and a wise woman withal, sought to heal Horus of his wound; but he remained motionless and stirred not. Loudly Isis lamented, bitter tears she shed. But all was unavailing; tears and lamentations could not restore life to her boy.

As she sat on the ground, rocking to and fro in the bitterness of grief, her sister Nephthys passed by. With her was the scorpion goddess, Serqet.

"What aileth thee?" asked Nephthys. "Wherefore this show of grief?"

"Alas!" cried Isis. "My boy is dead. My beautiful Horus is taken from me." And her tears broke forth afresh.

"Dead!" exclaimed Nephthys. "Dead! Of what hath he died?" Her voice shook with distress and tears sprang to her eyes, for the merry boy had endeared himself to her.

"This evening," said Isis brokenly, "when I came home, lo! he lay on the floor, dead, stung by a scorpion under the spell of Set; and now mine only treasure is taken from me."

Nephthys turned to Serqet. "Here is work for thee," she said briefly.

"Nay, 'tis too late for my power to avail aught," answered the goddess. "Had Isis invoked my aid before, I could have stayed the scorpion from touching her son. But 'tis not mine to rule o'er life and death. That power belongs to Ra the Mighty."

"'Tis even so," replied Nephthys. Then, turning to her sister, she said, "Isis, call on almighty Ra, our father. Beseech him to hear thee, and to restore life to thy son."

So at dawn, as Ra came forth from the vale of Amentet and entered the Boat of Millions of Years, the prayer of Isis rose up through the morning mists to heaven. With words broken by tears and sobs she begged the Maker of all Things to listen to her cry of woe. By Typhon's cruelty her beloved Osiris had been foully slain; she had been driven out of home, a wanderer on the earth; and now she had been robbed of her only child. "Give him back to me, O Ra," she cried. "Thou who holdest the keys of death and life, hearken to my prayer, and let not my son, mine only son, be reft from me."

Thus did she give words to her grief; and as the sorrowing company gazed with awestruck faces up to heaven, a miracle was revealed to them. The prayer of Isis reached the ears of Ra, and the boat was stopped. Thoth, the god of knowledge, descended to earth, and once again he stood before the exiled Queen.

"Ra, the Mighty One, life, strength, and health to him! hath heard thy prayer, O Isis," he said. "Hearken to his words. 'Thou goddess, thou who hast knowledge how to use thy mouth, behold, no evil shall come upon the child Horus, for his protection cometh from the boat of Ra. I have come this day in the Boat of the Disk from the place where it was yesterday. When the night cometh the light shall drive it away in the healing of Horus for the sake of his mother Isis.'"

At first Isis had been too astonished to speak, and now, without a word, she led the god to the couch whereon lay the body of her son. Pointing silently to the huddled form, the tears coursing down her cheeks the while, she whispered, "Is it not too late? Yet no, thou hast power over all things and thy word is the word of life. Heal him, I beseech thee."

The Persecution by Typhon

"Fear not, Isis," said Thoth, "and weep not, O Nephthys; for I have come from heaven to save the child for his mother."

The god bent over the body of Horus, and quickly spoke the magical words of power; when lo, what a transformation! The rigid limbs relaxed, the formless body waxed round and firm, a ruddy tint spread over cheek and face, and there—yea, it could not be mistaken—a smile played on the dimpling lips.

"Thy boy is thine again," said Thoth, turning to Isis. "Take him, and give thanks to Ra, the Mighty One, that he hath heard thy prayer; and know that he is ever mindful of the righteous."

With a cry of rapture Isis sprang to the couch and clasped the boy to her heart. For the moment the world was forgotten in her intense joy; then, remembering, she turned to thank him who had brought the answer to her prayer. But Thoth had gone, and even now the Boat of Millions of Years was speeding on its way.

VI. THE SECOND RESURRECTION OF OSIRIS

The time had come when Isis must begin anew the search for the body of Osiris, but ere she started out it behoved her to find some safe refuge for her son. He was proof against all hurt from man or beast or creeping thing; but any of Typhon's creatures, should they find him, might seize and carry him off, bringing further sorrow upon her. She went therefore to her sister Nephthys, and asked counsel of her.

"In sooth," said Nephthys, "what better home couldst thou find than with Ahura on the floating isle ? Besides ourselves, she is the only one who knoweth its secret. 'Tis unlikely that Horus's life will be endangered again, but, should such a mischance occur, he will be safer there than elsewhere, for at a word he can be borne far away from it."

"True," replied Isis. "Set is so wickedly cunning that I know not whether he may one day find out some countercharm to my enchantments. On the island my boy will be safe."

So next morning the two sisters sailed down the river to Busiris. Against the farther bank they saw the enchanted isle, and bespoke the boatman to cross over thither, but this he stoutly refused to do.

"That island is not of earth," he said in answer to their remonstrances. "There live the spirits of the dead. No man can touch its shores and return alive. Anything else ye ask of me will I gladly do, but that I cannot, dare not do."

"As thou wilt. Put us ashore here," said Nephthys ; and, having rewarded the man for his labour, she dismissed him.

"'Tis so much the better," she said, when he had departed. "If that be the tale told in this neighbourhood, it is unlikely that the whereabouts of Horus will ever become known to Set."

"Even so," Isis answered. "Call, I prithee, on the woman of the isle."

The Persecution by Typhon

Nephthys rounded her hand, and through it her clear voice rang out across the water. "Ahura! Ahura!" she called.

"Who calleth for Ahura?" cried a woman, descending to the water's edge.

"One born of heaven and earth, whom thou knowest. Come quickly," was the reply.

Soon the island could be seen approaching the shore whereon they stood, and in a brief space the two women and the child could step upon it. The woman who had spoken to them was very old, but her face was pleasant to look upon, for it was ever wreathed in smiles.

She fell down in silent adoration before her visitors, but Isis, stepping forward, raised her. "I see thou knowest me," she said. "But I am not come for worship. Hearken carefully to my words, for on thy scrupulous obedience hangeth more than thou wottest of."

Briefly she explained the purpose of her visit, giving many injunctions for the safe keeping of Horus; and then, bidding her son a tearful farewell, she moved away to the shore.

"Remember," she said, looking across the pretty wooded island, with its grove of trees and bubbling spring. "Remember, and guard him well from all scathe and ill."

"I will remember," replied the woman. "No harm can touch him here. Behold!" And the island quickly receded from the bank until it stood in midstream.

132 Egyptian Gods and Heroes

One last look and Isis turned her back upon the island; and so began her second search.

First she made a boat of reeds, light and strong, which she covered well within and without with pitch The reeds were of papyrus, and that is why the Egyptians said that a crocodile would not touch anyone in a boat made of this plant, for, in honour of the goddess, all papyrus things were sacred. When the boat was quite finished, she launched it and sailed downstream.

Difficult as the other quest had been, it was nothing compared to this. The baleful Typhon had dismembered the body of his brother, and had buried the fourteen pieces into which he had cut it up in diffcrent parts of Egypt. By this he hoped that it would be impossible to find them all and so to restore the body of Osiris a second time to life. What wonder if Isis felt nigh to despair, knowing neither where nor how to begin!

At every town she passed through she inquired of the people for any sign or token that might lead to the discovery of some limb or member, and wherever such was found, she erected a beautiful temple over the spot and placed therein a golden image of the god. The limb was carefully wrapped in linen cloth woven by herself and Nephthys, and Nephthys' son, Anubis, embalmed it so skilfully that it never decayed nor changed. Often, however, long weeks and endless months dragged slowly by with no success, and at such times the heart of Isis grew heavy within her.

The Persecution by Typhon

One eventide the boat drew in to shore near a large town called Abydos. The sun was setting in a sea of crimson and gold; the sandy hills, brown and bare by day, were bathed in its warm glow, that swiftly changed to blue and purple; the grey river gave back the vivid colours of the sky in red and scarlet, yellow and orange, blue and purple, and a score of delicate tints; the glaring white of the houses and temples on the bank was toned down to a quiet grey; even the ugly outline of the mud huts was softened, sharing in the witchery of the hour. For as the Sun-god sinks to rest he leaves his blessing on the land, transforming the monotony that pains the eye and crushes the mind into a picture of most gorgeous hues.

The calm of the scene stole in on Isis' troubled soul, and lulled it to rest. Her eyes lost the far-away look that was wont to dwell in them, and began to wander idly along the strip of sand beside the river. A shaft of light struck full upon a gilded dome and was reflected, a radiant bar of purple flame, across the palm-trees to the beach. There it ended in a ball of living fire, from which shot out rays of such dazzling brightness that the two women had to shade their eyes to look.

Suddenly Isis stood up in the prow, staring hard at the fiery ball; then she sprang to the helm and ran the boat on the beach. Leaping out, she hurried forward, and a moment later threw herself upon the sand.

Quickly the sunset light faded away, and darkness stole over the earth; but the wonderful thing on the sand glowed on. It seemed alive, and, now the sun had gone, to be the fount of light itself. But these things Isis heeded not, for there had she found the head of her lord Osiris.

In gratitude for its recovery, Isis built a magnificent temple in Abydos, on the site of the building whence had been reflected the ray of light that had guided her to the treasure. To this temple, which became one of the most famous throughout Egypt, she presented two granite statues of Osiris and herself; and on the highest pinnacle, so situate that it should catch the first rays of the rising sun and his last rays as he sank to rest, was placed an image of the god in purest gold.

What need to follow the goddess in all her wanderings? Day followed day, and one week succeeded another, as failure and disappointment became more frequent. But never again did despair loom dark and frowning. The finding of Osiris's head had filled her with a faith in her ultimate success that could not die, and resolutely she pursued her quest.

At last the long and trying search was ended, the separate limbs had been assembled, and the dismembered body of her husband lay in the boat. With her faithful sister in attendance, Isis returned to the Delta and the papyrus swamps, where she reverently laid the body on the sands beside the river, and repeated over it

The Persecution by Typhon

the magical words taught her by Thoth. The wondrous scene that once before had hallowed the dreary reaches of the Nile was re-enacted in all its awful solemnity; and, in virtue of her power as a goddess, to which was added a woman's love, Osiris was again made whole.

CHAPTER IX
The Work of Horus

I. THE PREPARATION OF HORUS

IT was many years later. The little boy who had been left on the floating island had grown a tall man, of mighty frame and giant strength. None could hurl the spear so true to the mark as he, none draw the bow with such unerring aim ; in wrestling-bouts he was more than a match for acknowledged champions, and at quarterstaff he beat all adversaries from the field ; his skill in swimming and diving was beyond compare, and his fleetness of foot had become a proverb. Fearless, manly, and just was he withal, and gifted with his father's power of winning all men's hearts to him. Such was the youth Horus, son of Isis and Osiris.

As yet the Prince knew nothing of his high destiny. He had been brought up a humble peasant, and it was chiefly among the peasants that his days at first were passed. But he soon attracted the notice of the elders of the town, and the wise ones were not slow to recognize that in the noble and kingly-looking youth, who had come so mysteriously into their midst, was

The Work of Horus

some one higher than of peasant blood, one superior to themselves; and ere long Horus became a welcome guest to each and all, were he governor or peasant. Every door was open to him; every house cried forth a greeting.

Now when all these things had been accomplished, Osiris deemed it wise to tell his son of the mission that lay before him; so one evening, after the day's work was done, he called the lad to him.

"Didst see the soldiers that passed this way to-day?" asked Osiris.

"Yea, my father," replied Horus. "'Tis said there is war in the lands of the south, and they are going to help the King's troops."

"It will be many days before they reach the capital," said his father, "for they must walk all the way. If thou wert a soldier, what animal wouldst thou think most serviceable to thee?"

"A horse," promptly answered the boy.

"Why?" queried Osiris. "Why dost thou consider a horse more serviceable than, say, a trained lion?"

"Because," answered Horus, "though a lion is more useful to a man that needs help, the horse is better for overtaking and cutting off an enemy. And that is what the true soldier should be doing rather than seeking help," he concluded.

The father smiled, and looked with pride at his noble and fearless son.

"And what is the most glorious deed a man can do?" he asked, after a pause.

"To avenge the injuries done to his father and mother," straightway replied the youth.

For a while the elder spoke not, and his eyes, full of fond affection, seemed to read his son's heart. "Sit down beside me," he said at length. "I have somewhat to say to thee."

Then Osiris told his son the story of his life in Thebes, and his work among the people, whereby he had gained their love and reverence; of the coming of Typhon and the shameless monster's deceit and treachery; of his cruel murder and the usurpation of his throne. As he went on to describe the wanderings and sufferings of Isis, her first success and his second murder and mutilation by Typhon, and the tyrant's indignities and cruelty to her afterwards, the face of Horus grew black with anger; his eyes blazed, his hands clenched, and his whole frame trembled with the wrath that seethed within him. But never a word did he speak. In silence he listened to his father's story, drinking in every word until he had grasped the full measure of the usurping tyrant's crimes.

"And now," said Osiris in conclusion, "the time draweth nigh when the reckoning must be paid. I cannot stay with thee. The gods call me home. To thee, my son, mine only son, is entrusted the work of avenging the wrongs of thy father and the indignities of thy mother. But I know that our honour will be restored.

From my new home I shall watch over thee and thy coming struggle, well aware that I do not watch in vain. Thou wilt go forth to war, in the knowledge that thou art fighting for right and truth, and, keeping that aim alway before thee, thou must win."

The two men stood up and looked each other in the eyes. Then the younger dropped on his knee, and, taking his father's hand, he bowed his head and kissed it.

"I will win, my father," he said.

II. THE DAY OF RECKONING

The barge of silken sails sped swiftly up the stream, this time not draped in black as when it bore the body of Osiris, but in dazzling white; and the three who sat silent beneath the thick canopy at the helm watched the passing banks with unseeing eyes. What thoughts were theirs on this last voyage together! Sweet memories of happy hours spent in this quiet solitude, darkened ever and anon as the sinister figure of their arch-enemy crossed the mind; but that grim spectre was quickly put aside, and when they spoke 'twas only to recall some glad remembrance of the days now past.

Quickly the boat sailed on. There lies Buto, a great city even in those early days; now over in the east can be espied the temple pinnacles of that which grew to be the mighty city On; then on the opposite bank a few mud huts, the site of future Memphis, unaware of its high destiny. At none of these do they pause;

and not until the golden statue of Osiris, that crowns the temple at Abydos and casts back the rays of Ra in streams of living fire, comes into view, does Horus, at a word from his father, turn the helm to the western bank. Here, before a deep cleft in the hills, the boat is made fast, the little party step ashore, and Osiris breaks the stillness with these words.

"The hour hath come to bid you both farewell," he said. "Would I might have tarried to complete the work I began, and purge this land of evil. But it hath been willed otherwise and I must go. To thee, my son, I bequeath all godly power, and here invest thee with the title 'Son of Ra,' in whose might shalt thou prevail over all thine enemies. Go forth, then, and do that thou hast to do, strong in the knowledge that Ra will always be with thee. And I, too, shall watch to protect thee from peril. Fare thee well, my son. My noble boy, farewell."

His eyes dimmed with tears, Horus looked up into his father's face. "Farewell, O my father," he said. "Verily I will live worthy of the name and honour thou hast given me."

Then Osiris and Isis moved toward the hills. "And to thee, O my wife," he said, "to thee who hast been so brave and unselfish and true must I also bid farewell. But never for a moment do I forget thee, and I await the hour when thou shalt join me again."

"Must it be so, my beloved?" said Isis brokenly. "Have I always to find thee only to suffer the pangs of parting? Can I not come with thee whither thou art going?"

"Not yet," replied Osiris. "It may not be. The gods have ordained that I join them now; but for thee there is still work to do here. Yet 'tis only for a season, and then shall I return for thee, and there shall be no more partings and no more tears."

"'Tis hard," moaned the woman. "'Tis hard to lose thee again, my husband. But the will of heaven be done."

"Farewell, my loved one," said Osiris softly. "'Tis not for long. But lo! The Sun-god waiteth for me, and I must go. Again, farewell." And with a last embrace they parted.

As he neared the cleft in the hills the Boat of Millions of Years sank lower and lower until it filled the gap, and when Osiris reached it a figure stood up and raised him into the boat. A moment later the watchers by the river saw him near the helm, and beside him stood the Sun-god himself. Stretching forth his hand Osiris spoke. "My blessing is with you," he said, "and my care shall be to watch over you always. And Ra biddeth me send his blessing too."

Then a deep, rich voice spake through the evening air, the words swelling like the music of a mighty organ into endless waves of mellow sound. "To those who have been faithful unto the end, even unto death, shall be given a crown of everlasting life and happiness. Ye weep now, but joy cometh in the morning, and glad shall be the awakening. Trust ye and fear not." And as the Sun-god ceased, the Boat of Millions of Years glided on into the night.

. . . .

After Osiris had left them, Isis and Horus sailed on for many days, pausing not until they came to a land far to the south.

Now it happened that Ra, in virtue of his omnipresence, had taken upon himself the shape of man, and had come to rule this land on behalf of his son. At that time Typhon was in the Delta, the papyrus swamps of which formed a home more to his taste than the drier plains of the south. Moreover, the inhabitants of that part, groaning under his yoke, and longing for the restoration of Osiris's rule, were only awaiting an opportunity to break out into open revolt; so for the nonce the monster had to leave the southern lands to their own devices.

But in the country yet beyond, called Nubia, there lived a race of savage barbarians who preferred the lawless rule of Typhon to the orderly government of Ra, and these set his authority at naught. Thereupon Ra entered their territories, quelled the uprising, and captured and slew the rebel chiefs. Then he returned to Edfu, whither Horus had come, and requested him to go and complete the work of conquest.

Horus had not forgotten the heavenly powers bestowed upon him by his father, and forthwith flew up to heaven in the form of a winged disk of the sun.

From his lofty station he espied his father's enemies again massing together, wherefore he descended and fell upon them with such fury as to rob them of their senses; and they, panic-stricken, attacked and slew one another. Horus then returned to the boat of Ra, who proposed that they should journey on the water to the scene of battle.

It must be remembered that in those days there were giants in the land, who often possessed miraculous powers. When Ra and Horus went down to the river, certain of their enemies, noting their movements, changed themselves into crocodiles and hippopotami and entered the water. Crocodiles, as you know, are more at home in water than on land, and hippopotami nearly so. In this guise, therefore, they hoped to take the two gods at a disadvantage.

The weapons of the dwellers in the Nile valley, like those of most primitive people, were at first sharp flints, such as can be seen in any museum to-day; but Horus had discovered the use of iron, and had armed his followers with spears and arrows tipped with this metal. Nor was it long ere the weapons proved their superiority and worth.

When the army of Horus perceived the enemy in the water, they went eagerly forward to the attack. In addition to his spear each man had a long iron chain. The spears they hurled at the beasts, and those they hit and maimed were afterwards bound with the chains and brought to shore, where they were slain.

But some of the enemy had escaped and fled to the north, and Horus followed in hot pursuit. Several minor conflicts took place, in which the rebels were routed with much loss, but it was not till they had reached the town of Dendera that another pitched battle was fought. Here, after waiting a whole day and night, Horus perceived his foes approaching, and, falling upon them, routed them with great slaughter.

Then followed a long chase, the foe ever fleeing toward the north before the relentless god. When they reached the Delta, they hurried to the palace of Typhon and offered to fight under his banner. The tyrant, angered by the open flouting of his authority in the south, had already prepared to march thither, and to crush these troublesome people once for all. But the advent of the fugitives from Horus changed his plans. Here was his old enemy, reborn in the son, come into the very heart of his own dominion. First, therefore, would he meet the usurper and blot out his race from off the face of the earth.

Now the spies of Horus had brought him word of the mighty force awaiting him, and he sent swift messengers throughout the land, bidding those who adhered to the house of Osiris to gather round his standard without delay. Meanwhile he went to see his mother Isis, who was at that time on the floating island near Busiris.

"The hour is come," said Horus, after they had warmly greeted each other. "Typhon awaiteth me, and

Horus in Battle

The Work of Horus 145

the trial must anon be made. Of the success of our cause I have no fear; but, lest I fall in the fight, I come to say farewell."

The mother took her son in her arms. How tall he was, how strong, how fearless! And how noble in all his thoughts! He was truly his father born again, and her mind flew back to the days when she and Osiris were young together.

"I will come with thee, child," she said suddenly. "Fear not for me. I shall be safe; and I would see the end of mine enemy."

So the two set out for the field where the issue was to be decided. Loud shouts of welcome greeted the return of the leader; then the warriors, seeing who was with him, bowed to the ground in silent adoration. Nor would they rise until Isis had given them her blessing for the coming fight.

Early next morning the forces of Typhon came in sight, and without delay Horus began the attack. So sudden and terrific was the shock that many of the tyrant's forces fled in dismay; but he, by dint of words and blows, urged the rest into the press of battle, which now raged furiously on all sides.

Fierce and terrible was the conflict. Now victory inclined to this side, now to that; at one moment it seemed that Horus had won the day, then the towering figure of the evil one rushed forward with tenfold fury, and, by the wondrous might of his arm, drove the enemy before him. For two long days the fight was waged, and yet the issue lay in doubt. The third day dawned, and as the sky blushed rosy red beneath the Sun-god's gaze, the opposing forces were locked together in a last deadly struggle.

All day long the battle lasted and the sunset flame had already begun to tip the distant hills, when Horus came face to face with Typhon.

"At last, thou murderer," he said. "Now is come the day of reckoning, and the score shall be paid in full."

"At last, thou son of my hate," roared Typhon. "Now will I slay thee, and utterly destroy thee and thine."

Their spears met. Fiercer and fiercer the weapons clashed, and gradually the two armies ceased their strife to watch the terrible duel. Breathless they stood, with eyes only for the giant forms fighting in their midst. This way and that the rivals reeled under the shower of blows they rained on each other. Now Horus is down, and mingled cries of exultation and dismay burst from the watching hosts. But instantly he springs to his feet, with resolution undiminished. Back and forth they sway, to right and to left, the vantage with neither. But his lusty youth and greater nimbleness are beginning to tell in Horus's favour, and Typhon is showing signs of weariness.

The Sun-god in his boat is fast nearing Manu, and soon will have entered the dark vale of the Tuat. His rays are flashed back from the glinting spear-points,

The Work of Horus

his crimson sea dyes all the field in blood. Now he rests on the mountain-peak, and looks down on the close of that Titanic struggle. At this moment the long spear of Horus is hurled forward. Swifter than the lightning flash it goes, and catches Typhon off his guard. Through shield and corselet it cleaves its way, piercing him to the heart; and with a groan that shakes the earth the giant falls, as a cry of frenzied joy bursts from the followers of Horus. Calmly the youth steps forward, and, drawing forth his spear, looks down on the evil face at his feet. But the lips speak not, nor the features change; for Typhon is dead, and will trouble the land no more.

Ancient Rulers of Egypt

OZYMANDIAS OF EGYPT

*I met a traveller from an antique land
Who said : Two vast and trunkless legs of stone
Stand in the desert. Near them on the sand,
Half sunk, a shatter'd visage lies, whose frown
And wrinkled lip and sneer of cold command,
Tell that its sculptor well those passions read
Which yet survive, stamp'd on these lifeless things,
The hand that mock'd them and the heart that fed :
And on the pedestal these words appear :
" My name is Ozymandias, king of kings :
Look on my works, ye Mighty, and despair !"
Nothing beside remains. Round the decay
Of that colossal wreck, boundless and bare
The lone and level sands stretch far away.*

P. B. SHELLEY.

CHAPTER X
The Builders of the Pyramids

I

WHILE most other peoples were still groping in darkness, the dwellers in the Nile valley had evolved a civilization, with a religious faith and a form of government more perfect than can be found among many nations of the world to-day. They cultivated the land, for which a network of canals was dug; they built houses and palaces, the splendour of which has never been surpassed; and they erected magnificent temples to their gods, of such grandeur and dignity that they became the marvel of the world. But of all their achievements the strangest, the most stupendous, and the most unchanging are the three enormous piles that stand near the head of the Delta, known as the Pyramids.

Of pyramids in Egypt there are many, but it is these three to which men's thoughts turn when the Pyramids of Egypt are spoken of. Standing on the very margin of the desert, where the rich black earth is cut off as with a knife from the region of limitless sand, they tower into the air like mighty fortresses set up to guard the land from the unknown hosts of the wastes beyond. But for a far different purpose were they erected. It was not defence against external attack that inspired their construction; it was defence against enemies from within.

Nearly six thousand years ago there lived in Egypt a king named Khufu. He was more powerful than any king had ever been before, and he gathered around him the wisest and cleverest men in the land. His sons were taught in all princely accomplishments, and some of them were given to learn the duties belonging to the office of priest, which included knowledge that then was looked on as magic.

One day Khufu's son, Herutatef, who was himself one of the most skilled magicians at court, told his father of a certain man who lived in Tet-Seneferu, who had the power of fixing again to the body any head that had been severed from it. "And moreover," added Herutatef, "the creature is as whole as it was aforetime."

"That is interesting," said Khufu. "In sooth, a man like that might be very useful to me. Thus, were a mistake made and the wrong man executed, as chanced but lately, he could amend the fault. Not that the accident imports much, but 'twould avoid complaints from the hapless man's kindred. Methinks there are possibilities in this magician of thine, Herutatef. We must have him here. Who is he, and where doth he live, sayest thou?"

"His name is Teta," replied his son, "and his home

The Builders of the Pyramids

is in Tet-Seneferu. But I doubt me he will not come, for he is very, very old."

"If he refuse we will fetch him, and teach him courtly manners," said Khufu, who was somewhat rough of speech.

"Think you he will care for threats?" answered Herutatef. "A magician as powerful as he can laugh even at kings."

"Well, offer him a bribe; tell him we will give him silks and fine robes, gold, a palace, anything, do thou but bring him hither," replied the King petulantly. "Hasten, I pray thee, for thy words have made me impatient to see him work his black art."

So the expedition set out, with Herutatef in command. When they arrived at Teta's house the old man came out to meet them.

"How fares my lord the King?" he said. "Health and strength be upon him!" Without waiting for a reply he went on, "I am even now ready to return with you, and will start forthwith when you have eaten. Enter, the board is spread for you."

Herutatef, too wise to betray surprise at the ancient magician's knowledge of their coming and its purpose, entered the house and sat down at the table. A royal banquet had been prepared, and when the feast was ended the party went down to the barge moored to the bank. In due time they reached the great city, and the Prince hastened to introduce the aged seer to his father.

"I am told," said the King to Teta, "that thou canst restore the head to a decapitated body and recall the dead to life. Is it so?"

"To restore the dead to life belongs to Amen alone," replied the old man. "But in uniting the severed parts of a body I have some little skill."

"Well," said the King, "here at hand are a few men to test thy parts. Bring them in," he said, turning to one of the officers; and half a dozen wretches, manacled and chained together, were led into the hall. "To show me thy power," he added to Teta, "the heads of these miscreants shall be cut off, and thou shalt join them to the bodies again."

"Nay, O King," answered Teta, "it is not well to play thus with fate. I promise naught, and it might chance my power would fail in this. Let a bird or an animal be brought, I pray thee, on which my poor skill can be shown as well as on these, our fellow-creatures."

"What matters it?" returned Khufu. "They are all prisoners, convicted of many crimes and shameless. If thou failest, haply the executioner will be spared a public task to-morrow."

"But not all have merited death, O King," answered the sage. "Bring me some creature of less value than these, I beseech you."

"That will be difficult," said the King grimly. Nevertheless he commanded that the magician's wishes should be granted, and a goose was brought into the hall.

At Teta's command the head of the bird was cut off,

and the body laid on one side of the hall and the head on the other. This done, the magician arose and began to utter strange words and incantations, which none there understood. As he spoke, the two parts of the goose began to move, approaching ever nearer together, until at last they were side by side. At a sudden exclamation from the old man the head leaped upward to its place on the goose's neck, and the bird straightway began to cackle and run about the hall.

"Splendid!" cried the King, and "Splendid!" cried the courtiers, who pressed forward to see if the goose were really whole, or if their eyes had been bewitched.

"Bring another bird," ordered the King, "and let Teta try again."

So a second bird was brought, and the experiment was as happy as before. Then an ox was treated in like fashion with the same success, and other birds and beasts, until his Majesty had had enough.

"Thou shalt stay at our court, Teta," said the King to the seer, "and all the honours of a prince be paid to thee. Thy knowledge pleaseth me well, and verily I have need of a man like thee." And so it was arranged.

II

You may have gathered from this tale that Khufu, or Cheops as he is sometimes called, was a selfish and somewhat cruel king, and as years rolled on his nature did not improve. Early in his reign he began the wondrous work which bears his name, and in course of time its grandeur and stateliness became the absorbing passion of his life.

"My ancestors have cut themselves stately tombs in the solid rocks," he said, "but I will erect a monument that shall be a fitting memorial to my greatness, and a tomb for my remains that shall live until time is no more."

So the work of building the Great Pyramid was begun. For years an enormous army, sometimes numbering more than 100,000 men, were engaged upon the colossal task. The hills across the river afforded ample material for the main structure, and the quarries in upper Egypt supplied the granite with which the inner chambers were lined. The huge blocks of stone, some of them weighing several tons, were floated down the Nile on specially constructed rafts to a point opposite the site of the future pyramid.

But how were they to be dragged to this position? Between the river and the site was a stretch of soft earth, in which the giant blocks would have sunk of their own weight. A road had therefore to be constructed from the river to the desert, along which the materials could be conveyed. This in itself was a task no less stupendous than the building of the pyramid, occupying ten years in its construction, but it was necessary if the grand design of the King was to be carried out.

So many men were taken from their rightful labour to work upon the King's affairs that not enough were

Hauling Blocks of Stone for the Pyramids

The Builders of the Pyramids 157

left to till the land and reap the crops, wherefore the people suffered many hardships other than the heavy toil to which they were subjected. They complained, too, of the endless demands of the King upon them, saying these were so exacting that they had no time to attend to the worship of the gods. "Let the temples be closed," replied Khufu, and it was done; and closed they remained for over a hundred years. At length, after more than twenty years of toil and sorrow, the last stone was laid in place, and the pile was finished.

Picture to yourself a field over twelve acres in extent. Covering this is a four-sided pyramid of nearly solid masonry, each side of which is more than one-eighth of a mile in length, and whose summit is higher than the highest building you have ever seen. Such is the Great Pyramid as it meets the traveller's gaze.

The entrance on the north side was closed by a huge stone revolving on a hinge, and so beautifully wrought that when closed it could not be distinguished from the other stones of the face, the alinement being perfect. From it a long narrow passage leads downward to a room deep under the centre of the pyramid; but before this chamber is reached there stands a massive granite door, which erstwhile closed the entrance to another pathway that led upward, first to a large hall, and thence from its two ends to chambers, one in the centre line of the pyramid, the other a little to the south-east of it. The one is known as the Queen's Chamber, and is exquisitely fashioned; the other is the King's Chamber, and in it lies the polished granite coffin of Khufu—empty.

Where is the body of the mighty King who had this funeral pile built? Here, enclosed in the huge mass of stone, it was to be safe against every desecrating hand; but, were it ever put there, it has long since been removed. It is said that the inhabitants, driven to frenzy by the tyranny of this King and his son, swore to drag their remains from their resting-place and tear them piecemeal, for which reason they were buried in a secret grave, known to few and soon forgotten of all. This, however, is not probable, for so cunningly had the entrance been concealed that over 1000 years had passed away ere it was found by robbers who sought to steal the jewels buried with him.

But whatsoever hap befell the founders, there the Pyramids remain, towering up to heaven, defying the ruthless hand of time, seeming fixed and enduring as the spheres above, a lasting monument to the greatness of their creators.

III

Near the Great Pyramid are two others, like to it but smaller. The second pyramid was built by Khefren, kinsman to Khufu, a ruler who carried on the evil practices of his predecessor, and reaped as bitter hatred from the people. Together these two reigned one hundred and six years it is said, during which time the Egyptians suffered every form of indignity and hardship

The Builders of the Pyramids

The third pyramid, though the smallest, was the most beautiful. In length and height it is less than half that of Cheops, but it was originally faced with polished stone, the lower courses granite, the upper limestone, and the blocks so nicely wrought and cemented together that the whole seemed one enormous shining stone. Unhappily the rulers of Egypt in the eleventh century A.D. sought to destroy all these monuments, and started out to deface the majestic work, a task they nearly accomplished before being compelled to abandon their work of wanton destruction. In one of the inner chambers, when the pyramid was opened, were found the granite sarcophagus and wooden coffin of the builder.

This king, Mycerinus by name, was son to Khufu, but a man of very different mould. Disliking the unjust and evil ways of his forbears, he commanded that all who had been working for them should return to their homes, and that the temples should be reopened and sacrifices made. His righteous judgments brought him honour throughout the kingdom, and for all these reasons he became the most beloved of all the kings of Egypt. When any man complained that his cause had been misjudged, the King asked him what he would have; and, if his case seemed good, he gave orders that he should be recompensed out of his own private treasury.

After he had been some years on the throne, there was noised abroad from the city of Busiris a prophecy telling that the King should die after six more years.

This coming to his Majesty's ears, he sent a messenger to the city, to expostulate with the oracle who delivered the prophecy.

"My father and my uncle," he said, "did evil in the eyes of heaven; they oppressed the people and outraged the gods; yet they both lived long in the land. I have ruled well; justice hath been in my right hand, and mercy in my left; yet now am I to be cut off in my prime."

"It is because thou hast ruled justly that the gods have decreed thy sway must end," came back the answer. "They willed that Egypt should suffer every kind of misery for the space of one hundred and fifty years, which thing the two former princes thy fathers understood, and helped to fulfil; but thou hast disregarded the will of heaven and must give place to another. When six more years are spent the time allotted thee will end."

"We will see," said the King to himself. And anon he gave command that henceforward the whole of each night was to be given over to revelling and enjoyment. Every night the palace and grounds blazed with torches; banquets were given, and entertainments of every kind were provided. Nothing that might add to the King's pleasure was forgotten. In this way, by turning the nights into days, he hoped to convince the oracle of a mistake, for thereby he would have enjoyed double the time granted him by heaven.

A curious story, still believed in by some Arabs of to-day, is told of this third pyramid. It was haunted

The Builders of the Pyramids 161

by the spirit of a beautiful woman, who lured men to their destruction by her charms. At about the going down of the sun she came forth, and any man she saw and wished to ruin she smiled upon so winningly that he forgot all else for love of her, and wandered about the country trying to find her. Many men have been observed wandering around the pyramid at about the hour of sunset, deprived of their senses, the victims of her charms.

This woman, it was said, was a famous queen, named Nitocris, whose husband was ruler of Egypt. But having incurred the wrath of some of his nobles, he was slain by them. To all appearance Nitocris did not mind this, and she showed no ill will to his murderers. Her feasts were as rich as before, and her amusements as wild and unbridled.

One day she invited all those Egyptians who had had part or lot in her husband's death to a great banquet to be given in a grand apartment underground. When asked why she chose this place for her feast, she replied that the room was to be consecrated, and the banquet was a part of the ceremonies. But in the midst of the meal, when the merriment was at its height, Nitocris secretly ordered her head servant to open certain sluices communicating with the river Nile by underground canals, and the room began rapidly to fill with water. The guests, brought to their senses by this peril, sought to escape, but none could find the door; and, turning to look for Nitocris, they discovered that she was gone.

162   Egyptian Gods and Heroes

In vain they fought and struggled to get out. Penned securely in this chamber underground, they all were drowned, victims to the Queen's revenge.

Nitocris, knowing that she would be punished for the vengeance she had wreaked, forestalled her subjects. Going to a chamber which had been heated previously by a fierce fire within, she threw herself into the ashes and was consumed.

Another story is told of this third pyramid by some who believed it was built by the King for his wife.

A certain lady named Doris had gone out one morning into her garden to bathe. The bath was open to the sky, and while she was in the water an eagle, soaring high overhead, noticed her bright jewelled sandals and, swooping down, carried one off. The royal bird flew southward until it reached Memphis, the capital of the country. By this time it had no doubt discovered that the brightest things are not the best to eat.

As it passed over the royal palace, where the King sat in open court dispensing justice, it decided to get rid of its useless burden, and dropped it. The sandal fell in the lap of the King, who, albeit much surprised at its sudden appearance, took it in his hand and closely examined it. Struck with its delicate proportions and exquisite beauty, he resolved to find out whose sandal it might be, and straightway dispatched

The Builders of the Pyramids 163

envoys to that end throughout the length and breadth of the land.

In each city to which they came the royal proclamation was read, offering large rewards to anyone who should point out to the King's emissaries the lady to whom the sandal belonged, and great honour to her if she came forward of her own accord. Many great ones came to claim the pretty thing, some, having heard what it was like, even bringing another to match it. But when they came to try it on, one and all had to be refused, for the sandal always proved too small.

At last the messengers arrived at the city of Naucratis, where again the proclamation was read out, and, as they were growing desperate at their want of success, they hinted that the King would give much more than was mentioned in the reward were his wishes gratified. But two days passed by, and none of those who came could show a foot to fit the sandal.

On the third day an old woman, worn and bent, came to the chief of the King's messengers. "Dost thou seek to try on the sandal?" he asked; and the men around him laughed.

"No, that do I not," she replied, "though perchance my foot would not be so far amiss as thou dost think. Howbeit the sandal is not mine, and I seek not to claim it. Yet it may be that I can earn the reward."

"Why, knowest thou whose it is?" asked the officer.

"I can guess," answered his visitor. "Hast thou asked the lady Doris to try it on?"

"The lady Doris! Who is she?" said the man.

"The most beautiful lady in Egypt," was the reply. "But she seldom walketh abroad, and of a surety would not come hither on such a quest."

"Where doth she live?" inquired the officer, all alertness.

"In the palace near the river at the north side of the town," said the woman.

Without waiting for further parley, the officer dismissed his visitor, buckled on his armour, briefly told the minister who accompanied the mission what he had heard, and all rode off in full state to the house to which he had been directed.

"Is this the house of the lady Doris?" he asked of the porter, clattering up to the gate.

"It is," replied the man. "But she receiveth no visitors unless they come invited."

"Tell her," answered the soldier, "that I come on urgent business from the King."

At the mention of the royal name the man bowed to the ground. "I will give my lord's commands to my lady," he said.

After some delay the company were ushered into a large hall, where the escort remained, while their officer and the minister entered the private apartment of the lady they sought.

"My servants tell me ye bring a message from the King," she said. "What can the King have to communicate to me?"

For answer the minister took out a copy of the royal proclamation. "Will you permit me to read this, lady?" he asked courteously, and she nodding assent, he read it through.

"Wherefore come ye to me?" she asked, when he had finished. "The proclamation is public, and might be for a hundred thousand ladies in Egypt."

"Methinks we have tried almost that number," said the minister with a smile, "and without success. Chance directed our steps to you, and I pray you will be good enough at least to try on the sandal." On the words he drew forth the glittering slipper and handed it to her.

Smiling pleasantly, but saying never a word, she took the proffered sandal, and, bending down, slipped it on her foot. The two men cried out in wonder, for it fitted perfectly. Then, before they could speak, she turned to a small chest, and drew out another sandal which she put on the other foot. To their amazement were added admiration and delight, for the second sandal was the exact counterpart of the first.

"May Ra be praised!" they cried.

"Will my lady accompany us back to Memphis?" asked the aged minister, with great deference. "'Tis the King's wish. Moreover," he added in a lower tone, "I think when he sees my lady, his honours will exceed even his promise."

So next day the party set out for the capital, travelling in almost regal state, and duly arrived at the royal palace. When the King saw the lady Doris he was enchanted with her great beauty, and soon afterward made her his wife.

For this Queen, it is said, the third pyramid was built; but whether for her or for the King matters little. At the expiration of his appointed time Mycerinus died, and was buried amid general sorrow in the mighty tomb that bears his name.

CHAPTER XI
The Riddle of the Sphinx

RISING out of the sand in front of the Pyramids is a great human head carved in stone. The features have been much damaged, chiefly by the Mameluke rulers of Egypt, who wantonly used it as a target for their weapons; but, in spite of this and the ravages of time, the face still gazes forward across the rolling flood and sandy wastes as it has gazed for untold centuries. Calm and impassive it is, a smile that seems sometimes of scorn, sometimes of pity, playing round the lips, a look of infinite wisdom in the never-closing eyes. To countless thousands in ages long gone by it was an object of devotion and worship; to one and all of the innumerable multitudes that have since looked upon it, it has been an object of admiration and wonder, to most, of awe.

What is this figure, and when and how came it there? It is the Sphinx, an image representing the god Horus, of whom you have already read something; but when it was carved no man can certainly tell. Some say that when the Pyramids were young, the Sphinx was old; that long, long before those mighty tombs were built, the mysterious smile and the human eyes had inspired reverent homage in the hearts of beholders: nor has it to-day lost aught of its mystical witchery.

But what it is and why it was made, wise men have learnt something. What is seen on approaching is a colossal head standing seemingly on the sand, but careful search has shown that this is not so. The whole figure is in the likeness of a man-headed lion, lying down with paws outstretched before it, and all hewn from the solid rock. The body of this monstrous creature is 150 feet in length, the paws 50 feet, the head 30 feet, and the height from the paws to the crown of the head about 70 feet. The face was erstwhile painted red, and on the head reposed a crown embellished with the sacred uræus, the symbol of divinity and immortality. Only traces of these now remain, but sufficient to prove that they added to the majesty of the god.

Often the Sphinx has been covered over by the ever-shifting sands of the desert on the edge of which it stands. Even in the days of the building of the third pyramid it had become almost entirely buried. In later times yet less care was taken to keep it clear, and gradually it was overwhelmed in the sea of sand.

A curious story is told of a king of Egypt and the Sphinx which you may like to hear.

Thothmes was a prince of the royal house, but not the direct heir to the throne. He was thus not concerned with affairs of state, and often went out on long

The Riddle of the Sphinx 169

expeditions for hunting and pleasure. In his chariot he drove two horses that were fleeter than the wind, and he was wont to set out with but two attendants, no man knowing whither he had gone.

On one of these hunting-trips he was separated from his friends, and, growing weary from his wanderings and the heat of the day, he lay down in the shadow of the Sphinx and fell asleep. In his sleep the god Horus-Ra appeared to him.

"Thothmes," called the god.

The Prince looked up in some surprise, and at first did not recognize his visitor; but as soon as he did so he hastened to make obeisance to him.

"Thothmes," said Horus again. "The throne of Egypt is not thine inheritance, yet, because thou hast faithfully observed the laws of Ra and ever been duteous to the gods, thou hast found favour in their eyes and shalt be raised to kingly power."

Thothmes bowed to the ground.

"One thing thou hast not done," continued Horus. "My image lieth buried in the sand, and none of all thy royal house hath thought fit to free it, though in the time of thy fathers it was reverenced by king and people alike. Now the sand whereon it hath its being hath closed it in on every side, and none honoureth me enough to make it clear as of yore. Say unto me that thou wilt do this thing, and I shall know that thou art verily my son and he that worshippeth me."

"The wishes of my lord are the commands of his servant Thothmes," said the Prince.

"Be it so," answered the god. "Draw nigh unto me, and I will be with thee, and I will guide thee." With these words Thothmes woke up.

As the god had spoken, so it came to pass; Thothmes succeeded to the throne and ruled wisely and justly over Egypt. He was as good as his word, too, and had the image of Horus cleared of the sand that submerged it, and commanded that homage should be paid to it as in the days of old. Moreover, between the mighty paws he built a small temple, in which were recorded the circumstances that had led to its construction.

Another temple, much larger and considerably earlier than this, lies a few yards to the south-east of the image. For this reason it is usually called the Temple of the Sphinx, although it is of later date than that figure, and is probably connected with the building of the Pyramids. Its walls and columns are of alabaster and red granite, much of which is beautifully polished and most carefully wrought. This was also covered with sand, and only in the last century was it found again and the sand removed.

But beautiful as is the temple, stupendous as are the Pyramids, wonderful in their magnitude and perfection as are all the monuments of ancient Egypt, there is none that possesses the strange fascination, the mysterious enchantment of the quiet face that for un-

The Riddle of the Sphinx

numbered centuries has watched the eastern horizon to greet the first faint rays of the rising sun, and whose inscrutable smile has given birth to the expression, 'The Riddle of the Sphinx.'

CHAPTER XII
The Guardians of the Desert

ABOUT 3500 years ago there ruled over Egypt a powerful king named Amenhotep. He had conquered the whole of Egypt, parts of Nubia, and Sinai, and a goodly portion of Asia also owned his sway. In gratitude to the gods for their protection and favour he built a great temple at Thebes, called the House of Amen, the remains of which lie near the modern village of Luxor, from which it now takes its name.

This temple was about 500 feet long and 180 feet wide, and consisted of a large central court surrounded by a colonnade of triple columns; and from it a long avenue of sphinxes led to a still grander temple at Karnak. Its greatest glory, and that which makes it still in some respects the most beautiful of all the temples, was the aisle of tall columns, seven on each side, leading from the great court to another at the northern end, where now stand two colossal granite statues of a later king. These columns are built of huge stone blocks, their capitals being wrought to represent the flower of the papyrus; and nowhere does

The Guardians of the Desert 173

the architecture of ancient Egypt give a greater sense of dignity and strength.

Afterward Amenhotep resolved to honour himself as well as the gods, and, having built another temple on the west bank of the Nile, he erected before it two colossal statues of himself, now known as the Colossi of Memnon. Standing on pedestals twelve feet in height, they tower up some sixty feet more; and, when first built, were crowned with the crown of the two Egypts, that rose several feet higher. Each made of a single block of sandstone, they were set up at the foot of the low hills that shut off the fertile valley from the wastes behind. There they stand to-day, defaced by the ruthless hand of time, it is true, but rearing aloft their heads to heaven with a sense of calm superiority, as if they are, indeed, the guardians of the desert.

In those enchanted days when miracles and other wondrous deeds were wrought, it was not long ere strange powers were discovered in the statues. One of them, it was found, could sing, and the man who rose betimes would be rewarded by hearing it chant its mournful note. Just after sunrise it began, and for a space the silence of the desert was broken by the tender song of the statue—so soft and gentle that no one would have guessed it came from the mighty form overlooking the plain.

Nor was the story all imagination, for on many a sunny morn, as Ra stepped into the Boat of Millions of Years, the early visitor might hear, issuing from the northern statue, the sound of harpers plucking gently on their strings. When the Greeks visited Egypt they were struck with the strangeness of the occurrence, and in their poetical way soon supplied a story to explain the mysterious sounds.

The statue, said they, was an image of Memnon, an Ethiopian prince who went to help the Trojans in their great war against the princes of Hellas. When he was slain by Achilles, Memnon's mother Eos, goddess of Dawn, went about the earth mourning his loss. On reaching the statue at Thebes she was moved by its resemblance to her valiant son, and remained to weep over it ; and the sounds heard every morning were the cries of grief uttered by the goddess for her son.

Many famous men of ancient times travelled to Thebes to hear the marvel, several of whom left a record of their visit in the poetical inscriptions scratched on its base. The best known of these visitors was the Roman emperor Severus, who, in gratitude for being favoured by the statue with its song, resolved to repair the damage that had been done to it by an earthquake about a hundred years before, when the upper part had been cracked and thrown down. Stone was brought from the hills hard by, and several layers were placed in position until the injury was quite repaired. But the statue was not grateful for the emperor's attentions ; indeed, it seemed as if it resented his desecrating hand, for it became as silent as its brother, and from that time forth the sounds were heard no more.

CHAPTER XIII

The Builders of the Temples

YOU have read of the great temple at Luxor, and of its beauty and grandeur; but there is one still more imposing in its extent and strength, albeit less beautiful in design and execution. This is the temple of Karnak, really a series of temples built by successive kings in honour of Amen, god of gods at Thebes. Once the two temples of Luxor and Karnak were connected by an avenue of sphinxes, over a mile in length, but, excepting a small part near to Karnak, all traces of these figures have long since disappeared.

One entrance to this temple was through a gateway of stone, sixty feet in height, the walls of which were sculptured with figures of men and gods, and at the top was carved the winged uræus, and painted in divers colours. This gateway still stands intact, but quite detached from the ruins of the temple beyond.

But on solemn feast days, when king and priest and all the greatest of the land would come in grand procession to pay honour to the gods, another gate afforded entrance to the temples. A broad avenue, lined on either side by sphinxes, led up from the river to a thick, high wall, the pylon of the temple, as it was called, from which, a hundred feet above, the flag of Egypt proudly waved. A high and massive door gave access to a courtyard, at the farther end of which was another similar wall, with a kind of porch before it. On either side of the porch stood a tall statue, carved from a single block of granite, of Rameses II, the king more famous than any other in Egyptian history. This second doorway led into a vast hall, usually called the Hall of Columns.

Picture before you a room nearly 120 yards long and 60 yards wide, the roof supported by one hundred and thirty-four massive columns. These columns are not all of the same size. Twelve of them, running down the centre of the hall, are 68 feet high, and so thick that six men with arms outstretched could scarce encircle one of them. The remainder are not quite so high or thick, yet huge enough almost to make one feel that here must be a temple built by the gods themselves, and no mere handiwork of man. The columns are carved with sacred writings, cut on a correspondingly vast scale, some of the characters being as long as a man.

On the outer walls of this hall are cut inscriptions that tell of the wars in which the kings who built it, Seti I and Rameses II, were engaged. The latter was a very boastful king, and it is to be feared he arrogated to himself many of the deeds of his equally warlike father; but some of the incidents are full of human

The Builders of the Temples

nature, and the pictures one and all are remarkable for their truth to life.

This king, Rameses II, had a favourite lion, which he had nourished and brought up from a cub, and wherever he went it went too. In his wars the King in his chariot, with the lion by his side, struck terror into the hearts of his foes, and on many an occasion the animal did him yeoman service by leaping on the enemy and tearing them to pieces.

Rameses II was deeply devoted to the worship of the gods, and the treasures of gold and silver and precious stones that he received as toll and tribute from his various vassal states he employed in either finishing temples already begun or building new ones, and endowing them with fitting revenues. He took great care, however, that his own exploits should be duly recorded in the inscriptions that decorated the walls, and his martial deeds, often highly magnified, are carved on almost all the temple walls of Upper Egypt. In each temple, too, he set up statues of himself, always carved from a single block of granite.

The grandest of these, the largest statue ever found, was erected before the entrance of another temple on the western bank of the Nile. It was sixty feet in height and weighed nearly 1000 tons. Of this sculpture an ancient writer says, "It is not only commendable for its greatness, but admirable for its cut and workmanship, and the excellency of the stone. In so great a work there is not to be discovered the least flaw, or any blemish whatsoever." When we remember that it was cut from a single block of stone, which had to be transported hundreds of miles from the place where it was quarried before it was set up, our admiration of the ingenuity that must have been displayed is yet more increased. Unhappily, the Persian conquerors of Egypt threw it down from its lofty station, overturned and broke it, and otherwise wrought much damage upon it.

Beside this image of the King was another smaller statue, and both were seated in chairs of state. Behind them, and adjacent to the front wall of the temple, were four more statues, these all standing. Like the greater one they were damaged by the Persians, the heads being broken away from the bodies.

Other places at which this mighty King built or finished temples are Abydos, where he completed the work begun by his father, Seti I, and Abu Simbel in Nubia, the temple which, hewn out of the heart of the mountain, is the greatest of all his works. A long flight of steps leads to a courtyard, at the farther end of which is the temple wall, 100 feet wide and 90 feet high. On each side of the entrance are two seated colossal statues of the monarch, each 60 feet high, that have been cut out of the solid stone.

On a tablet in this temple one of the best accounts of the war waged by Rameses against the people of Kheta in Asia is found. This nation, after having been reduced to a state of subjection and made to pay tribute

The Builders of the Temples 179

by former kings of Egypt, now thought fit to throw off the yoke and defy the King of the two lands of the north and south to do his worst.

In great wrath the Mighty Bull, as Rameses loved to call himself, gathered together his forces and marched against the unruly tribe, resolved to quell them utterly. Having crossed the sandy deserts of Sinai, he came to the city of Kadesh, and there he pitched his tent.

Now it chanced that two spies of the army of Kheta were caught by the Egyptian troops, and these were brought before the King as he sat upon his throne.

"Who are ye?" said he, in a thunderous voice.

The unfortunate spies deemed it best to tell the truth. "We are spies of the chief of Kheta," said they, "sent to find out where thou art, O King."

"And now ye know, I hope," answered the King grimly; and the two men, having not wherewith to reply to this, wisely held their peace.

"Where is this knave ye call King?" continued Rameses. "It hath come to my ears that he lieth in the town of Aleppo." Aleppo lay several miles to the north; and thus had it been spoken by two men who had before come into Rameses' camp to spy out the strength of the Egyptian forces; and they, pretending fear and a desire for the protection of the great King, had deceived him, and so had been allowed to depart.

"Behold," said they, "the chief of the Kheta, with all the hosts that he has gathered under him, that are in number like to the sands of the seashore, stands ready to do battle against thee behind the city of Kadesh."

"Is that so?" said the King in surprise, and he called for the officers engaged on outpost duty.

"These men tell us," he said sternly, when the officers were brought before him, "that the wretched Kheta chief is even now without the walls of Kadesh, and not in the neighbourhood of Aleppo as ye have reported to us. Wherefore have we not been told the truth?"

"O King," faltered one at last, "when we sent word unto you, the Kheta chief was, as we said, at Aleppo."

"Since when, methinks, ye have been all asleep," said the monarch, growling like a lion in his wrath. "But why, then, were we not kept informed of the hordes this low-born chieftain hath amassed to fight against us?"

"To us they seemed not so large as these spies declare," replied the officer; "and we knew thy might, O King, was more than a match for all the caitiff creatures of this Khetan chief."

These words of flattery probably saved the officers from immediate execution, for, after looking closely at the men for a moment, Rameses turned to his guards and said, "Take them into safe keeping until we are resolved what punishment is meet for them."

As soon as they were removed the King bade preparations be set afoot for an immediate attack upon

Rameses II defeating the Khetans

The Builders of the Temples 181

the enemy. But the ruler of Kheta had meanwhile outflanked the Egyptian army, and unexpectedly fell on the rear with such vigour that the Egyptians turned and fled. At this sight Rameses raged like a wounded bull, and, seizing his lance, he commanded his charioteer to charge straight into the ranks of the foe. So swift had been the movement that his men had no time to follow, and the King found himself hemmed in by the surging hosts of his enemies.

In these straits Rameses called on the god Amen, and prayed him to come to his help. "To thee, O Amen," he cried, " have I dedicated temples, and filled them with gold and silver and sweet-smelling woods; for thee have I brought great stones from the lands of the south wherewith to build to thy glory; for thy honour have my ships traversed the wide seas and brought back the treasures of all lands wherewith I might adorn thy sacred places. Now am I forsaken of all my followers; I called unto them and they would not hearken. But thou, O Amen, art more to me than millions of warriors, and hundreds of thousands of horses, and tens of thousands of brothers and sons: the deeds of the hosts of men are as naught, and Amen is better than they all."

Then the King saw the hand of Amen outstretched to him, and heard a voice saying, "Lo, I am with thee; my power is with thee, and I am more than hundreds of thousands united."

Hearing this Rameses charged the foe, and they fell

before him like corn before the scythe; they sank under his blows, and when they fell they never rose again. The Khetan chief, observing the havoc wrought, turned and fled, leaving his troops to fare as best they might. But the King's charioteer, seeing the hordes that lay between the monarch and his men, was afraid, and begged his master to retire from the contest.

The King laughed. "Why fearest thou, Menna?" he cried. "Shall we shrink because the rebels are gathered against us? My enemies shall be slain, and trampled underfoot like the dust of the earth. Come, charge again."

A second time the King dashed into the ranks of his foes, and a third, and a fourth. Six times did he cleave his way through the opposing host and pass out scatheless. Then the men of Kheta, broken and scattered by these furious assaults, turned and fled, and Rameses was master of the field.

When he got back to his troops he reproached them for their cowardice in not coming to his support. "Menna," he said, "alone remained true to me, and for his faithfulness I hereby decree, in presence of you all, that henceforth he shall be captain over all my horsemen."

It is pleasant to think that Rameses did not forget his two brave horses through whose aid he had won the day, for he further commanded that, when he was in his palace at Thebes, their fodder should always be given them in his presence, whereby he might be sure they received the care that was their meed.

CHAPTER XIV
The Lady of the Obelisks

I

BEHIND the Hall of Columns at Karnak is another part of the same vast temple, the part that formed a centre round which the rest of the numerous courts and temples were built. This small hall holds little of attraction in itself; but at the farther end stand two giant pillars, in a way more wondrous than the columns in the great Hall of Rameses.

These two pillars are called Obelisks. They were not the first, nor are they the only ones of their kind, but they are the grandest and the most famous that ever were set up. One of them has fallen, shaken by an earthquake, but the other still tapers skyward as proudly as when it was first erected. Its height is almost one hundred feet, and, like its companion, it is a monolith, that is, a single stone, " and has in it," says the ruler who put it there, " neither join nor division." The tops of both were once covered with gold, but that was stolen long ago.

Just think of it. A single stone of solid granite, one

184 Egyptian Gods and Heroes

hundred feet in height, polished smooth and crowned with gold, "towering up among the pillars of this venerable hall," as the ancient record says, so that "they should pierce the sky." Where did they come from and how were they put up? This story will tell you.

In the days of old, long even before Rameses was King, a Princess was born in the royal house of Thebes. There was nothing very remarkable in that; many princesses had been born before, but this one was different from all the rest. Indeed, it was said that her birth was miraculous, and that when it took place, Amen, the chief of the gods, called all the other gods around him and asked each one to give her a blessing. "In her," he said, "I will unite in peace the two lands of Egypt, and I will give her all lands for her dominion. Bless her, therefore, and make her rich and prosperous."

The gods, of course, did what Amen desired, and when the Princess was born she was gifted with all the virtues that woman could possess.

When she was about twelve years old, Hatshepset—for that was the Princess's name—was taken into the temple to undergo a ceremony of purification at the hands of the gods; and, the rites having been duly performed, they each renewed the promises they had made at her birth, and added others too. "We bestow life and peace upon Hatshepset," they said to Amen. "She is thy daughter, and she is adorned with all thy qualities. Thou hast given unto her thy soul and thy

The Lady of the Obelisks

words of power and thy great crown. Whatsoever is covered by the sky and surrounded by the sea thou makest to be her possessions."

With these and many other blessings did Hatshepset start out in life, and it was not long before she began to show her power. Her father took her on a journey in which they traversed Egypt from one end to the other, receiving homage and admiration from all the people. Nor were they unmindful of the temples, and in many cities they carried out long-needed repairs and made additions to the places of worship. In several of the shrines they thus visited the promises of great glory to come to the Princess were repeated by the gods, who also foretold what she would do when she came to reign.

On their return to Thebes the King resolved to make his daughter co-regent with him, that is, she should rule with him and be in all matters of government even as the King's majesty. This was not to the liking of the people, for they had never had a woman to rule over them, and they were fearful lest she should prove too weak to maintain the glory and prowess of their country. But the King turned a deaf ear to all objections, pointed out her divine origin, and commanded a large tent to be prepared where the coronation of his daughter should take place.

On the appointed day there were forgathered all the nobles and chief men of the empire. and ambassadors from many foreign countries, to do honour to the

Princess; while the common people were like to swarms of bees for multitude. Loud cheers, mingled with deep-throated shouts of welcome, burst from them as the chariots of the bidden guests dashed by, cries that grew to a mighty roar when the royal coach drove past. For, though they resented the idea of a woman ruling over them, they truly loved and revered the Princess.

When the monarch and his daughter had passed through the lines of assembled nobles and princes, they mounted the dais at the end of the tent and sat down in the chairs of ivory and gold. First were read the wonted speeches of welcome to the foreign envoys and their replies, and as soon as these were finished the King arose and ascended to the royal throne. Seating himself, he spake.

"Hereby," he said, "I set my daughter Hatshepset in my place and seat her upon my throne, and from this time henceforward she shall sit on the holy throne with steps. She shall give her commands unto all the dwellers in the palace, and she shall be your leader, and ye shall hearken unto her words and obey her commands." Then, standing up and looking defiantly around, he continued, "Whosoever shall ascribe praise unto her shall live, but he who speaketh evil against her Majesty shall surely die."

At the words the trumpets blared, and the heralds made the proclamation to the people without. Within the tent the nobles, on hearing the sovereign's words, cast themselves on the ground and swore fealty and homage to the King and his daughter, acknowledging her as their ruler, and then rose up and danced for joy, whereat the heart of the King was exceeding glad.

II

After the death of the King, Hatshepset during some years ruled alone, and although she married a prince who was looked upon as the sovereign, and who took to himself the credit of whatsoever was done, Hatshepset was the real ruler of Egypt. She used her power and ability wisely and well, and the people her subjects had no cause to complain that a woman and not a man held sway.

It was at this time that Hatshepset conceived the idea of setting up the two great obelisks in the temple, for a memorial to her father and to the glory of Amen. Her architect, Sen-mut, one of the cleverest men of his craft, was called, and, having received directions from the Queen upon the nature of the memorial, he sent armies of workmen to the quarries near Assuan to prepare it.

The huge stones were cut and shaped in the quarries, then moved on rollers to the river, where they were embarked on rafts and floated down to Thebes. Albeit they are so large and must have involved enormous labour, only seven months elapsed from the beginning of the work to the erection of the monoliths in the temple. There they stood, as they stood throughout long centuries, a monument not only to the glory of

Amen but also to the skill and craftsmanship of these early workers in stone.

"They shall be seen from untold distances," said Hatshepset in her decree; "and they shall flood the land with their rays of light, and the sun shall rise up between them in the morning, even as he riseth from the horizon of heaven. I, as I sat in my palace, remembered the god who made me, and my heart was moved to make for him two obelisks with copper and gold upon them, which should tower up among the pillars in this hall. This have I done that my name should abide permanently in this temple, and endure there for ever and ever." And her wish was gratified.

To the glory of Hatshepset there is yet another memorial to be recorded. This is a temple, said to be the most artistic of all these relics of the past. When she had been Queen for many years, she resolved to construct a burial-place worthy of her dignity and majesty, and bade Sen-mut prepare designs such as no king had ever known.

The result of his labours was the temple of Der-el-Bahari, a building about 800 feet in length, and consisting of three terraces, one above the other, built into the hillside itself. The upper one consisted of a series of burial-chambers; the middle one was a large hall extending deep into the hill, and formed the shrine of the god to whose glory the temple was built; while the third and lowest portion consisted of another series of rooms set apart for the service of the priests and for other duties connected with the temple worship.

The walls of this building are adorned with sculptures of the various journeys of Hatshepset through her kingdom, and of the expeditions made by her soldiers to distant lands. One of the most interesting of these was the voyage to a land called Punt, which is believed to have been the country whence came the gold and silver and precious stones that adorned the Temple of King Solomon in Jerusalem. The series of pictures tells very vividly the story of the Egyptian travellers, their reception by the King and Queen of Punt, the honours paid them, and the treasures of gold and silver, ivory and feathers and skins, precious woods and spices and incense that they brought back.

In this temple, after a long and happy reign, the great Hatshepset, "Child of Amen," was laid to rest; and if her temple was dishonoured by her successor, and in time became forgotten, this very forgetfulness preserved her remains from the desecration often shown to her more famous brethren, and left her undisturbed in her neglected tomb until long centuries had rolled away.

CHAPTER XV

The Journey of Khensu to Bekhten

IN the days of long ago there was a king of Egypt so powerful that he conquered all the neighbouring countries and even extended his rule far into Asia. Every year he sent his ministers to bring home the taxes collected by the governors of each district, and these were used both to enrich his treasuries and to improve his army for further warfare.

One year he resolved that, instead of sending the usual official, he would go himself to gather the tribute. Perhaps he thought he was being cheated; perhaps he wished to find out where next he could best pursue his conquests. Whatever his motive was, he had no sooner made up his mind than he sent for the Lord High Chamberlain, and bade him make preparations for the journey.

That worthy official put forward every objection he could think of against the proposal; for he was growing old, and it suited him much better to live at ease in the royal palace than to undertake a long and arduous journey. There were rumours of a rising among the people of the Delta, he said. " We leave our army to

Journey of Khensu to Bekhten 191

keep order," replied the King. One of the great religious festivals was at hand, said the Chamberlain. "The priests will perform the necessary sacrifices," answered the monarch. "Thou will be away many months," finally objected the official. "Is it wise to leave the kingdom so long O King?" "We shall be all the more appreciated when we come back," smiled his Majesty. A few days afterward the royal progress began.

As the Chamberlain had foretold, the journey took many months; but it was not quite so unpleasant as he had pictured. Everywhere the people flocked to the route they followed, to see the royal procession pass by. The gleaming armour of the soldiers and the gold and silver trappings of their steeds truly made a brave show, and the pomp and glitter of the Court attracted the humble rustics from far and wide.

At last they reached a large city, whither the chiefs of all the conquered tribes had been bidden to come, for there his Majesty, son of the Sun, would deign to meet them in person. To the brilliance which ever surrounded the personage of the King was added a note of quaint picturesqueness, as one chieftain after another took up his station about the royal tent. Fierce-looking warriors from the mountains of Armenia, clad in garments of fur; tall nomads from the deserts of Kheta, garbed in loose cloaks of red, blue, green, and yellow; grave and dignified elders from the east and from the west, with flowing robes of finest linen, mixed together in strange confusion. Men who at another time would gladly have flown at one another's throats shook hands in solemn friendship. For was not the King himself come in his might to see them!

On the day of audience the chieftains were assembled in the great tent of the King, and one by one came forward to lay their tribute at the foot of the throne. In addition to the annual sum demanded, they brought beautiful presents of gold and silver work, cunningly-wrought carvings set with rubies, turquoise, and lapis-lazuli, and sweet-smelling incense, myrrh, and sandal-wood.

When the King of Bekhten came to the throne, he had little to lay there except the usual tribute, and for a moment a cloud loomed on the great monarch's brow. But it speedily passed away, for this king was a faithful ally and had rendered him signal service in the past.

"We welcome thee to our presence, O Prince of Bekhten," he said, "and we would fain see thee at our Court. Why hast thou never come?"

"Your servant thanks you for your kindness," said the chieftain, "but he is old. Such a journey is not for him. Yet if you will accept a substitute, O King, there is one of your servant's house now here who is more fitting to accompany you."

"Let us see him," answered the King.

Thereupon the King of Bekhten made a sign to an attendant, who left the tent. In a few minutes he returned, leading by the hand a woman, closely veiled.

"If my lord will accept this representative," said the chief, bringing the woman to the seat of the King, "I pray you do me so much honour. She can wait upon the Queen, if my lord so wills. And she is considered somewhat beautiful," he concluded naïvely, as he drew back the veil from her face.

The King of Egypt started from his seat. Never had he seen such loveliness before. Of regal carriage and bearing, fair-skinned, blue-eyed, rosy-cheeked, with long black hair, she was very different from the duskier beauties of his own land.

"By the might of Amen," cried the monarch, "she shall be no waiting-maid. She shall be my Queen, and, in token of my troth, I take her now beside me in the presence of you all."

Descending to the woman he led her to the throne, seated her on it, and stood beside her. The simple grace of the action touched the imagination of the wild chieftains, and a great burst of cheering rent the air.

The festivities had now to be prolonged in honour of the King's marriage. When seven days had passed the procession set out for the land of Egypt, and in due time reached Thebes.

For many years affairs took their usual course, and the King and Queen were very happy together. One day the Chamberlain entered the royal presence and announced that an embassy from the lord of Bekhten craved audience of his Majesty.

"Let them enter," said the King readily.

"Who art thou, and why comest thou to our Court?" he asked of the leader, not unkindly, when the embassy had been ushered in.

"Your slave is the son of your servant ruling in Bekhten," answered the young man, "and I come here to crave a boon of our father."

"Say on," replied the monarch.

"Long have we known of the might of Egypt, and of the wisdom of its learned men," said the Prince. "Since the day when my lord honoured our humble house by raising a daughter to sit by his side we have learned much more. Now another daughter, the sister of her who shareth my lord's throne, lieth grievously ill, and all the skill of our land availeth not to cure her. Your servant, my father, therefore requesteth that a wise man of Egypt be sent that she may be made whole."

"We grieve to hear of our sister's affliction," answered the King. "We will see what can be done."

Straightway all the wisest men in Thebes, the doctors, physicians, and magicians, were assembled in the great hall of the palace. After much discussion they chose one of their number, named Tehuti, a man famed throughout the land for wisdom and learning, to accompany the Prince; and the embassy returned at once to Bekhten.

Three more years had sped their course, when one day the Chamberlain entered the King's presence to say that Tehuti had returned, and with him the Prince of

Journey of Khensu to Bekhten

the land. Without delay they were brought to the royal chamber.

"How fareth our sister of Bekhten?" inquired the monarch, after the usual salutations had passed. "We hope you bring a good report of her."

"It is because we are unable to speak well of her that we have hastened our return," replied the Prince. "The wise man whom you, O King, sent with us, saith that she is possessed of an evil spirit, against which the power of a god alone can prevail. Your servant, my father, craveth that you will send, therefore, one of the gods of the land of Egypt, of whose might he hath heard much; and perhaps the deity will have mercy on the daughter of your servant."

The King of Egypt was discomfited to hear of the continued illness of the Princess, for he knew that his Queen grieved exceedingly for her sister, and he was anxious to make her happy. At this season he was celebrating a great religious festival; so he went into the temple, and, standing before the image of the Moon-god, prayed to him. This god not only ruled the month, but had power over all evil spirits in earth and air and sea; and as it was these which attacked man and brought upon him disease, sickness, madness, and even death itself, the King invoked the aid of the god on behalf of the Princess of Bekhten.

"O my fair lord," he said, "once again do I come into thy presence to ask thy aid. Our sister of Bekhten lieth ill, and none can cure her. Allow therefore, I beseech thee, the god Khensu to go to Bekhten that he may heal her. Grant that thy saving grace may go with his divine Majesty, and deliver the Princess from the power of the demon."

As the King ceased his prayer the image of the god nodded twice, and he knew that the god gave his approval to the request. Indeed, the Moon-god later bade the image of Khensu to be brought before him, and, laying his hands upon it, he bestowed upon the statue a fourfold portion of his power and spirit.

The return journey to Bekhten was a far more magnificent progress than it had been before. A great escort of soldiers and many priests and followers accompanied the Prince, for it behoved them to show due honour to the god. At last, after seventeen months, they arrived at the capital. The whole army of Bekhten was drawn up on the plain outside the city, and the King himself, with all his nobles and chiefs, came forward to do homage to the god. Khensu requested that he might be brought without delay into the presence of the Princess, and the statue was placed within the sick chamber. Then the priests went out from before him, and the handmaidens of the Princess likewise left the room.

When they went back after two or three hours they found the Princess sleeping peacefully. A faint colour tinged her cheeks, and her lips curved in a gentle smile; so they knew that the evil spirit had departed from

Journey of Khensu to Bekhten

her. So speedy was her recovery that in a few days she was restored to perfect health.

"If this god is so powerful," said the lord of Bekhten to his chief counsellors, "he could help us against our mortal enemies too. Let us keep him here instead of sending him back to Egypt."

At this proposal there was great dissension among the courtiers. Some were in favour of it, others strongly against it. "You have received a great blessing from the Majesty of Egypt," said they to the King, "and now you would rob him of that which is his. Would you bring down upon us not only the wrath of the god himself, but also the might of the land of Egypt?"

Nevertheless the King's wishes triumphed, and the god Khensu actually tarried in Bekhten three years, four months, and five days. One morning, however, when the priests went into his shrine they found him not, and forthwith they reported his disappearance to the King.

The monarch was now greatly afraid, and messengers were dispatched in every direction to trace the statue. But it soon became evident that no mortal hand had been guilty of its removal. Several men told how in the early morning, just as the sun rose, they had seen a great hawk of gold fly up from the top of the temple, and, after rising high in the air and hovering for a few minutes above the city, its mighty wings gleaming so that they could scarce bear to look on it, the bird had turned away toward the south.

"It was the god Khensu," said his priests. "He wearied of staying in Bekhten and would return to his own temple in Thebes."

Then the King called before him the priests who had accompanied the god when he came from Egypt, and declared to them that he had always been desirous to return the statue, but no fitting occasion had presented itself. "Moreover," he added, "we sought to send with him such gifts as would show our gratitude for the favour he hath done us, and these have not yet been gathered. But bring the chariot of the god," he commanded, turning to his chief minister; "we will at least send those offerings that it lieth in our power to make."

So the chariot was brought and loaded with gifts and offerings of gold and silver and precious stones. Nor did the wise old King forget to reward with great riches all the priests and nobles who had come in the train of the god.

When they reached Thebes they found that Khensu had already taken up his abode in the temple, so the treasures were carried from the chariot and laid before him. But the god, knowing that his recent power was only a gift of the Moon-god, caused the offerings to be removed to his shrine, where they long remained.

CHAPTER XVI
In the Days of the Famine

THE life of Egypt depends on the great river that flows through its midst. Every year it brings down with it a mighty flood of water that formerly spread over the land, changing the low-lying districts into broad lakes. As the flood diminished the waters receded until again they were confined within the channel of the river, and, through the rich deposit of mud that covered the earth upon which the flood waters had lain, there sprang up wheat and maize and plants of every kind. But should the flood fail or be small in amount, want and suffering were the lot of the people.

The Nile flood issued from the island of Elephantine, in the far south, whereon stood the first city that ever was built. Thence, too, rose the Sun-god when he went forth to give life to man and beast and plant. In the centre of the island was a large, gloomy cavern, and here the tumultuous waters were held back by the god Khnumu. At the proper moment Khnumu drew back the bolts and threw open the doors, and the pent-up waters surged forth to fill the country with their bounty.

Now it chanced that once Khnumu was wroth with the people of Egypt, and refused to allow the Nile flood to perform its beneficent work. For seven years the waters failed, and the Egyptians were reduced to terrible plight. In his extremity the king, Zosiri by name, wrote to his viceroy Mater, who ruled the island and all the lands adjoining thereto, asking for information and help.

"By reason of the reports which are daily brought to us as we sit upon our throne in the royal palace," wrote Zosiri, "we are filled with sorrow, and our heart is stricken with grief for the calamities of our people. For seven years the god of Nile hath hidden his face from us; for seven years his waters have brought no life to the land. The corn from the storehouses is nigh exhausted, fruit and vegetables cannot be found, no green thing liveth on the earth, and the people starve for lack of food. So great is their need that men are robbing one another, and violence and outrage are rife. Children cry of hunger in the streets, the young men can scarce walk because of their weakness, and the old men, crushed to the earth, lay themselves down to die.

"Now we have remembered that on a like occasion in the days of our fathers, the son of Ptah, god of the South Wall, delivered the land from the enemy. But the son of Ptah is no more, and cannot come to our aid. Tell us therefore, O Mater, whence come the Nile and his waters, and who are the gods that watch over them."

"Methinks," said Mater to himself, on reading the letter, "that I shall do best to go to the King. Thus can I tell him what he desireth to know, and peradventure find some profit to myself in the event." And without more ado the governor of Elephantine and all the territories of the south set about his journey, and in due course arrived at Thebes.

The King was overjoyed to see him, and, in his anxiety to learn all about the Nile-god, almost forgot to wait until Mater had performed the customary obeisance. He gave him a seat beside the royal throne, bade him put himself at ease, and anon plunged into the subject he had so much at heart.

"Who is the god, Mater," he asked, "that ruleth the Nile, and why hath the flood failed us for so long?"

"The god of the flood," replied the governor, "is Khnumu, and he holdeth the water in check in the island of Elephantine."

"Where and how lieth this island?" asked Zosiri; for, although he ruled over it, he knew no more of it than its name.

"Elephantine is a beautiful isle in the midst of the stream," said Mater. "Above it lie the lofty rocks that form the outer breastwork of the great South Wall, and from the midst of which come the waters of the Nile; but the flood is concealed in a cavern in the island. The lands round about are not so rich as those of Thebes, yet they bring forth corn and wine and oil sufficient for the people's needs. On a knoll in the middle of the isle is a temple to Khnumu, but it hath fallen into disrepair; for it hath pleased the kings thy fathers to take away from him the lands that yielded him a revenue." Here the viceroy made a significant pause.

"What then dost thou counsel?" asked the King.

"The Ruler of the North and South knoweth what is best," answered Mater uncompromisingly; "but it might be well if my lord the King appealed to the god Khnumu in his own temple within this city."

"Thy words are the words of wisdom," said Zosiri; and that selfsame day he went into the temple and, after offering sacrifices to the god, knelt before him in his shrine. As he prayed Khnumu appeared unto him, and, raising his hand aloft, he spake.

"I am Khnumu the Creator," he said, "My hands rest upon thee to protect thee. I gave thee life. I am the guide and protector of all men. I am the god of the Nile who riseth in his flood to give health and life to those who toil. Behold, I am the father of all men, and the possessor of all the earth. Yet do men neglect me, and in their foolish pride do harden their hearts and call not upon my name, nor hold my holy fane in worship any more. Now inasmuch as thou hast come to me and besought my help, the waters shall rise as of old, and riches and wealth shall come upon the land of Egypt."

It was even as the god had said, and that year the Nile rose as it was wont to do in the days of yore.

In the Days of the Famine

King Zosiri remembered that the god had complained that his shrine had been left to fall into ruin, though stone lay nigh in abundance; and, in his gratitude, he gave command that it should be repaired without delay.

"To the great god Khnumu," he decreed, "we yield the sovereignty of all the land for two days' journey round about Elephantine. Henceforth tithes of all the produce of the earth, of corn, wine, oil, animals, birds, and fish, shall be delivered to the temple of the god. All precious stones, metals, and woods sent thence to other lands shall likewise pay dues for the maintenance of his shrine."

"And what reward hath my lord for his faithful servant?" asked Mater on the morn of his departure, as he slipped the roll of papyrus containing the decree into the folds of his gown.

"To our beloved servant Mater," said the King, "we entrust the collection and application of those tithes and dues; and we give him our assurance that, so long as Khnumu withholdeth his anger from us, so long shall he be free from our royal displeasure, whatsoever his enemies may urge against him."

CHAPTER XVII
The Treasure-Chamber of Rhampsinitus

I

USUALLY the kings of Egypt were as lavish in their bounties and as reckless in their extravagance as they were eager to gather treasure, be it in peace or war. They accumulated great riches, and distributed and spent them freely, a practice that contributed in no small degree to their popularity with their subjects. More than one king, on the complaint of some injustice from a poor subject, bade his ministers recompense the man from his own private treasury. But now and again a Pharaoh came to the throne who loved money above all other things, and played the part of miser in a position where every opportunity was offered for the amassing of wealth.

Rhampsinitus was a king of early Egypt. He had waged several wars against neighbouring tribes, and returned on each occasion rich in captives and treasure. His captives he put to ransom or sold as slaves, thereby increasing the wealth the wars had given him. This instead of spending he carefully put

The Treasure-Chamber 205

away. The spirit of greed was upon him, and his one ambition was to add to the pile of riches that was already greater than any king had hitherto possessed. But with the spirit of greed there always comes close on its heels another evil spirit, named Fear, which never allows the one possessed a moment's rest: he lives in hourly dread lest his heart's delight should be taken from him.

Now, albeit Rhampsinitus was a king, this evil spirit spared him not, and he grew afraid that the treasure he had so diligently amassed might be stolen and lost. Thereupon he sent for his architect and told him to construct a chamber such that it would be impossible for anyone to enter therein without his knowledge. A room was built adjoining one of the walls of the palace, and the stones were so cleverly hewn and so well cemented together that the most crafty robber would never have been able to effect an entrance. The architect, you see, was a very skilful man, so skilful, indeed, that the King himself knew not how cunning a brain he had. For he had guessed the purpose of this chamber, and had arranged one of the stones in such wise that it could easily be moved. By pressing upon a secret spot the stone swung noiselessly back as on a hinge, disclosing a cavity large enough to admit a man's body. But when the stone was closed, so well wrought was it and so truly laid withal, that had a man looked never so closely he would not have remarked any difference in that part of the wall from the rest.

In this chamber, then, the wealth of the King was stored. Chests filled with gold and silver, urns stocked with gems, and richly wrought baskets of wondrous workmanship, were heaped one upon another; and hither came Rhampsinitus almost every day to gloat upon their beauty and abundance.

It is easy to understand that the architect who built the room had designs upon the treasure; but, either from fear of being found out or from more honourable motives, he never made use of the secret entrance. Suddenly he was taken ill, and calling his two sons, Hophra and Sen-nu, to his bedside, he told them of what he had done, saying that it was for their sakes he had made this entrance, that they might never want. He then told them exactly the position and dimensions of the revolving stone, bidding them at the same time tell no man what they knew. Having thus made provision for his children, he soon afterward died.

II

King Rhampsinitus sat with head bowed in thought. Three mornings before he had gone to the treasure-chamber and found one of the boxes almost emptied of its coin; yet the seals upon the door were intact. That morning he had paid another visit, to find that an urn, containing great store of gems, had been despoiled of its treasure; yet were the seals unbroken, and the guard placed at the door swore that no one had come thither during the night. Clearly there was

The Treasure-chamber of Rhampsinitus

The Treasure-Chamber

treachery at work, and Rhampsinitus knew not how to cope with it.

Sorely perplexed, he struck sharply on the gong by his side. "Tell the Lord Chamberlain to come hither," he said to the Ethiopian who answered the summons.

The Chamberlain had barely roused him from his slumbers, for he was not wont to receive a royal summons at this hour without due notice. Fearing that it boded no good for him, he hurried into his robes, revolving in his mind all his doings of the past week in the effort to find a cause for such unusual proceedings. But the suddenness of the order, coupled with the effects of the previous evening's festivities, only confused his mind the more; and, with a sigh of resignation, he ceased to think about it, and entered the royal presence with as dignified and virtuous an air as he could assume.

"Ha, Ra-men-ka," said the King, "thou seemest somewhat ruffled this morning. Methinks thou keepest too late hours while the Prince of Nubia honoureth us with his visit."

"The cares of state, O King," said the Chamberlain, "are very exacting, and ofttimes detain me far into the night. There are many arrangements to be made for the pleasure and comfort of my lord's guests."

"Yea, indeed," replied the King drily. "Howbeit, 'twas not for that I sent for thee. Dost thou know that thieves have twice been into my treasure-chamber?"

The question came so abruptly that Ra-men-ka was more discomfited than before, and for the moment was rendered speechless with surprise. "Impossible, my lord," he faltered at last.

"Ra-men-ka," said the King gravely, "presume not to say I speak that which is untrue. I have said that thieves have entered my treasure-chamber, and I add that they have stolen an urnful of most valuable jewels."

"Imposs—" began the Chamberlain, when the glitter in the King's eye checked him. "Certainly, my lord," he corrected himself quickly.

"Certainly!" thundered Rhampsinitus. "Certainly! What meanest thou, sirrah? What dost thou know about it to speak so certainly?"

"Nothing, my lord," stammered the Chamberlain. "I was merely approving of what you said, O King."

"Approving, wert thou?" said the King shortly. "Then approve no more of what I say."

"O King, I will not," said Ra-men-ka meekly.

"Wilt thou not, in sooth?" replied Rhampsinitus, glaring at him. But he did not pursue the subject.

"Now hearken to me," said the King. "These thieves are no common robbers, for they have extracted the jewels and left no trace behind of their presence. The seals I put upon the door are untouched, and the guard hath seen no one. We must set a trap for them."

"Yes, sire," answered the Chamberlain. "I will have a small trap made such that it may not be noticed,

The Treasure-Chamber 209

and when the thief putteth his hand within the jar it will seize and hold him fast."

"Didst ever hear of the fox that was caught in a trap by the tail?" said the King.

"No, sire," replied the other.

"Once a fox was caught in a trap by the tail. He knew that unless he could get loose he would be killed when the hunter made his rounds next morning, so, although he sorely regretted the loss of his beautiful brush, he deliberately bit off his own tail and set himself free. The rest of the story is of no moment here, but dost not think thy thief would be like the fox?"

"But I propose to catch him by the hand," replied the astonished Chamberlain.

"Ra-men-ka," said the King, "henceforth must I insist that thou keep better hours, or the cares of state will prove too much for thy health. Dost thou know if the dungeon under the west court of the palace is in as unwholesome state as ever?"

"Seeing that no one hath been in it for several years, it is probably much worse," answered the Chamberlain.

"Ha!" said the monarch. "Well, thou must devise a trap such that when the thief cometh and toucheth an urn, it will catch him forthwith and hold him fast—arms, legs, and body. And hearken! Whether thou succeed or not, I am thinking of giving that dungeon an occupant."

And, musing over this dark saying, the Chamberlain was dismissed.

III

The two brothers, Hophra and Sen-nu, were planning a third excursion to the royal palace. Riches easily obtained soon disappear, and they were not long in squandering their stolen wealth.

" 'Twill be dark to-night," said Hophra; "we will fetch a little more from the treasury." And accordingly about midnight they set out.

Carefully they searched for the stone, pressed upon the secret spring, and, while Sen-nu remained on watch without, Hophra entered the treasure-chamber. But scarcely had he put his hand into one of the jars, when arms and legs and body were pinioned as in a vice, and he could not move a pace from where he stood.

"Brother," he called softly.

"Here am I," whispered Sen-nu. "What wouldst thou?"

"Come hither quickly," replied Hophra. When his brother had crawled in, pulling the stone almost to after him, "Behold," said Hophra, "I am caught in a trap, and I cannot get free. Canst thou aid me?"

Sen-nu struggled stoutly with the bands of brass that gripped his brother fast, but all to no avail. He tugged and pulled and threw his weight on the fetters, but they never yielded, and at length he stared at Hophra in despair.

"Now in truth am I caught," said Hophra. "But 'tis not needful that both suffer. When the guards enter the room on the morrow, they will easily guess that two men were here, and if they find me they will know thou wert the other. Take then thy knife, and cut off my head and carry it home. Thus shall no one know who I am."

Despite Sen-nu's remonstrances, Hophra insisted on this being done, pointing out that if they were both taken and put to death, their widowed mother would be deprived of her support, and this argument decided Sen-nu to carry out his brother's wish. Then he crept from the room, fitted the stone in its place, and went home, taking his brother's head with him.

When the King entered the chamber at dawn, the first thing that met his gaze was a headless man bound in the trap; yet, search as he would, he could find neither exit nor entrance to the chamber.

"This is passing strange," he said to the Chamberlain, who accompanied him. "But 'tis clear this robber had an ally whom we must catch. Let the body be taken and hung without the palace wall. Set a guard over it, with orders to seize anyone weeping or lamenting near it, and bring him to me."

In giving this command the King made manifest his wisdom; for, as you have read, to attain a future life it was imperative that a corpse should be buried with all due rites and ceremonies, and the monarch expected some one either to claim the body or at least to come and mourn over it.

When the mother learnt of the shameful exposure of

her firstborn, she wept bitterly and reproached her surviving son with cowardice. " Bring me my son's body," she cried, " or, by the gods of my fathers, I will go to the King and tell him all that thou hast done."

" How can I bring the body ? " said Sen-nu. " 'Tis guarded night and day, and anyone approaching it is closely watched. And didst thou tell the King, what would that avail ? Thou wouldst lose two sons then instead of one." But she refused to be comforted, and at length Sen-nu, yielding to her prayers, promised to fare forth to see what might be done.

Taking half a dozen asses, he loaded them with skins of wine and, as evening drew on, drove them along the streets toward the royal palace. When he came to the place where were the guards, he drew two or three of the skins toward him, and covertly untied the necks. The wine ran freely out, and he began to beat his head and breast, lamenting on the ill-luck that had befallen him; and the soldiers, seeing the mischance, picked up any vessel that was near, and, hurrying to the spot, caught as much of the wine as they could and eagerly drank it.

" Scoundrels, thieves, robbers," cried Sen-nu in pretended rage, " would ye seek to profit by my misfortune ? May ye perish, all of you ! Leave the wine alone, I say, leave it alone, or, by Amen, I will complain to the King of your knavery."

" What ! " cried the soldiers laughing. " Wouldst thou have us let good wine run to waste ? That would

The Treasure-Chamber 213

be folly. In sooth thou hast lost thy wit with the wine. We have taken nothing thou couldst have saved. Calm thy wrath and we will help thee to rearrange thy burdens better."

So with fair words they pacified him, until Sen-nu, forgetting his anger, began to talk with them, and one of them made him laugh uproariously. Then he offered them one of the wine-skins as a gift for their good fellowship, and sat down to drink with them. It was not long before the wine took effect, and one and all were chatting and laughing boisterously. Sen-nu presented the guards with a second skin of wine, and then a third; when, being drowsy from the heavy drinking, first one and then another fell asleep in the shade of the wall. Sen-nu, who had feigned to be as intoxicated as the worst, waited till it was quite dark, when he quietly took down his brother's body from the wall and bore it home to his mother.

As may be imagined, Rhampsinitus was sorely vexed at the second failure to catch the thief, and abused Ra-men-ka so roundly that that unhappy man would have resigned his office but he dared not. A third trick met with no better success; indeed, it brought public ridicule upon the King, and his Majesty was now weary of the task he had set himself. So he issued a proclamation which he commanded to be read in all the towns of his dominions, saying that he would pardon the offender and give him royal largess if he would but come forward and make himself known. He was not a little surprised when the selfsame day a man presented himself at the palace and declared he was the culprit.

The King bade him be brought anon before him. "Art thou not afraid," he said, when Sen-nu was led into his presence, "to come before me after all thou hast done?"

"The King hath promised me a free pardon," answered Sen-nu, "and he will not dishonour his word."

"Brave as thou art clever," exclaimed the King. "And in good sooth thou wert wise to trust to the word of the King. The pardon is thine, and more. I offered to reward the man who could prove to me that he was the culprit, and if thou dost this, truly thou shalt not regret it."

Then Sen-nu revealed to Rhampsinitus the secret entrance to his treasure-chamber, and proved that he was the brother of the dead man. So amazed was the King at the youth's sagacity and boldness that he gave him his daughter in marriage, and raised him to great honour in his house.

CHAPTER XVIII
The Reign of the Twelve Kings

THERE was a certain king of Egypt named Sethos, who sprang from the priestly class, and had gained the throne because of dissension among the people. One of his first acts was to take away all power from the military class, for they were to be feared more than all others beside, and he deprived them of the land allotted to each member by former kings. These indignities greatly estranged the warriors, and when Sennacherib of Assyria marched with his forces into Egypt they refused to fight against him. In this calamity King Sethos went into the inner sanctuary of the temple and called upon his god to come to his help. As he bewailed his hapless state he fell asleep, and dreamed that the god appeared to him and told him to be of good cheer, for he would send help when the time was meet.

Then Sethos marched out against the Assyrians at the head of an army consisting of farmers, artisans, and traders, and camped near Pelusium, a town on the eastern branch of the Nile that commanded the entrance into Egypt. Thither came the forces of Sennacherib;

216 Egyptian Gods and Heroes

and during the night, as the two armies lay waiting for the dawn, the one in fear and trembling, the other singing and vaunting their proud strength, countless multitudes of mice came up from the fields hard by into the Assyrian camp, and ate the bowstrings of the soldiers, and gnawed in twain the thongs of their shields. When they arose next morning they were helpless, and fled incontinently; and great numbers fell at the hands of the Egyptians. Wherefore King Sethos, on his return to Memphis, set up before the temple of Ptah a statue of himself with a mouse in his hand, and underneath was this inscription, "Look on me, and learn to reverence the gods."

But as years rolled on Sethos grew ever more disliked by his people, and on his death they resolved never more to allow themselves to be ruled by one man. This resolve they failed to keep in later years, but for the moment they were filled with zeal for their new plan. Wherefore they chose twelve kings, dividing the whole country into twelve districts and setting over each a king. The twelve were bound together by intermarriage, and they also took a solemn vow not to depose any of their number nor to seek aggrandizement at the expense of the rest. They were, you see, jealous of one another, and their distrust was heightened by the declaration of an oracle, which said that he among them who first poured out in the temple of Ptah a libation in a cup of bronze should become sole ruler of all Egypt.

The Reign of the Twelve Kings

As a means of strengthening their bond of union, the twelve resolved to build a monument which should serve both as a common memorial to them and as a burial-place for their remains. To this end it was said they constructed a wonderful building known as the Labyrinth, in the fertile spot of land called the Fayoum. This Labyrinth had twelve courts with gates exactly opposite each other, six facing north and six south. Round each court ran a colonnade of white stone, from which opened off chambers, and these led into other courts, and thence by fresh colonnades into other houses until the stranger was lost as in a maze. The total number of rooms was 3000, half of which were built underground, and the other half above ground and resting upon them. The upper rooms were for the use of the priests who attended to the temple worship and the many servants who ministered to them; the lower chambers were the tombs of the twelve kings and of the sacred crocodiles that were held in honour there.

Now it came to pass that on a certain day the twelve kings had met together for worship in the temple of Ptah at Memphis. All went well until the time for pouring out the libations, when it was found that by some mischance the high priest had brought out only eleven goblets instead of twelve. Psammetichus, who stood last in the line of kings, was thus without a goblet; but, not wishing the ceremony to be stopped, he took his bronze helmet from his head, saying, "This will do for my cup. Pour the wine within." As he spake the other kings looked quickly at one another, remembering the saying, "He that first among you poureth out in the temple of Ptah a libation from a cup of bronze shall be King of all Egypt"; and after the service was over, they met together in secret to consult what should be done.

"He is worthy of death," said one. "He hath taken an unfair advantage, seeking his own glory in spite of the oath we sware."

"In sooth," said another, "he was ever ambitious, and, knowing the oracle, he seized the opportunity, hoping to be made King over us."

Then arose a grey-headed old man, bent with years, and wise beyond all the rest. "Hearken, my brothers," he said. "Psammetichus hath indeed fulfilled the words of the oracle, but how know ye that it was with guilty intent? Had not all of you helmets of bronze on your heads, even as he had, and would ye have done otherwise had ye stood last? But call him in and examine him, and learn wherefore he used his helmet, knowing what the oracle had spoken."

So Psammetichus was called before them and they questioned him closely; but to all he stoutly protested that he had no thought of the oracle, and sought only to allow the religious service to go on uninterrupted.

"It was even as I told you," said the old man, when Psammetichus had been removed. "The finger of Fate is in this. Kill him an ye will, and the gods will exact a terrible vengeance from you. As for me, I lay no hand on him whom Heaven befriendeth."

At these words there arose much discussion in the council, some still cleaving to the wish to kill him, but the greater part inclining to the words of the wise old King. At last it was agreed that Psammetichus should be stripped of his kingship and banished to the marshes of the Delta, and forbidden to hold intercourse with any other part of Egypt.

For the second time in his life Psammetichus went into exile, he having been a fugitive when erstwhile the usurper Sabacos seized the throne and put his father to death. Now he fled into the marshes, where he lay hid for several years, hoping that a means would be found whereby he might return to his dominion. But, wearying of the loneliness, he sent to the town of Buto, where was the oracle of Latona, to inquire how he might take vengeance upon his enemies and regain his rights.

This oracle of Latona at Buto was the most celebrated in all Egypt, for never had it been known to err. Hence it was consulted from far and wide and its wealth increased daily. A magnificent temple was built in honour of the goddess, surrounded by a high wall, the entrance being through a massive gateway sixty feet in height. Rich sculptures decorated the walls, and gold and silver ornaments were there in great profusion. But the greatest marvel was a shrine dedicated to Latona, cut out of a single stone, each side measuring sixty feet in length and the same in height. The roof was formed of another flat stone, so large that it projected at the eaves six feet on every side.

Hither then did Psammetichus send his inquiry, and the answer came forthwith. "Vengeance shall come from the sea," said the oracle, "when brazen men shall appear." The cryptic answer puzzled the exile exceedingly; for never, thought he, could brazen men come to his aid, and from the sea withal.

Howbeit, not long afterward it came to pass that a number of soldiers, men of Ionia and Caria, were driven by stress of weather out of their course, and put in, perforce, to a small harbour on the Egyptian coast, where they disembarked and, being in want of food, began to harry the land. Tall and fierce were they, and, clad in armour of bronze, they inspired deep dread in the defenceless peasants and fishermen of the coast regions. One of these, who had fled on their approach, brought the tidings of their arrival to Psammetichus, and, as the rustic had never before seen men so clad, he said that brazen men had come up out of the sea and were plundering the land.

The King pondered on the news, and then light came to him. "'Tis the word of the oracle," he said. "The brazen men from the sea! I will haste to meet them." And without delay he set forth to find the strangers.

He had little difficulty in this, for the tale of their evil doings was bruited far and wide. On coming up with them Psammetichus entered into conversation,

The Reign of the Twelve Kings

and found out whence they came and how they chanced to be there. After long parley it was agreed that they should return to their own land and bring back a large force of warriors, and aid Psammetichus to gain his kingdom once more; in return wherefore they should have rich rewards and a city in Egypt to dwell in.

In a few months all was ready, and placing himself at the head of his new allies Psammetichus marched south. The conflict was short, for his enemies had received no tidings of the power which was being brought against them; and, after one or two engagements in which they were defeated, Psammetichus entered Memphis and was crowned King of all Egypt. Thus were the two oracles fulfilled.

In gratitude to the gods Psammetichus built a large gateway in the south wall of the temple of Ptah in Memphis, and also a court for the Apis bull. This court was adorned with a number of statues, and surrounded with a colonnade, resting upon statues each eighteen feet in height.

He reigned fifty-four years in Memphis, doing much to restore Egypt to her ancient prestige among the nations, and died full of years and honour; and his son Necho reigned in his stead.

CHAPTER XIX
The Shadow of the End

HOPHRA, the great-grandson of Psammetichus, was the last of the mighty kings of the ancient line of Egypt, for soon after his reign the country was conquered by the Persians and ruled by them. He carried the arms of Egypt into far distant lands, bringing under his sway kingdoms that had long since thrown off the Egyptian yoke; but, although he did so much for the glory of his land, he was put to death at last by his own subjects. And his untimely end came about in this wise.

Hophra had sent an army to subdue Cyrene in Libya, a rebellious town and a stubborn. Instead of gaining an easy victory as they expected, the Egyptians suffered a terrible reverse, so many being killed that the survivors and the relatives of those who were slain declared the King had sent them thither in the hope that they would be destroyed, when he could rule Egypt without fear, and inflict whatsoever measures of oppression he would. So, far from home, they broke out into open revolt.

When the tidings came to Hophra, he called Amasis, one of his most able men and a tried warrior, and bade him go see if he could win the people back to their allegiance by fair words and promises. Amasis thereon set forth, and on his arrival in the rebel camp he summoned the leaders before him.

"Wherefore do ye gather thus together, and set the King at defiance?" he said. "Is it for this that he hath raised you to be the chosen warriors among his people and given you lands and honour?"

"He gave us over to death," cried one; "for that he sent us to fight against Cyrene."

"Nay, friend, 'tis not so," replied Amasis. "If ye suffered defeat and loss, 'twas not the King's wish. Rather did he think to yield you the greater glory, trusting to your known valour to carry you to victory against any odds."

"Hark to my lord Amasis," said a voice. "Verily he would make a splendid wooer." And at the words there was a loud laugh.

"Thou speakest sooth, I hope," answered Amasis, "for I come hither to woo thee and these others to your faith. Lay down your arms and go to your homes, and I promise you the King's forgiveness for your treason here made manifest. No harm shall come to you, and the remembrance of your misdeeds shall be wiped out."

While he spake one of the soldiers had come behind him with a shining brass helmet in his hand, and at this moment he placed it on the envoy's head and cried, "Long live King Amasis! Hail to our King!" The cry, begun in jest, was taken up in earnest, and soon the men were beseeching Amasis to claim the crown himself, promising to go with him and support him against the forces of Hophra. At first Amasis demurred; but secretly he was pleased at the offer of a crown, and afterwards he agreed to march at their head and urge their claims on the King.

"If he refuse to hearken to your just complaints," said Amasis, knowing full well that it would fall out so, "then perchance I will give ear to your request."

While pretending to act for Hophra, Amasis travelled in royal state, and news of these doings being brought to the King, he sent Patarbemis, one of his most trusty friends, to bring the traitor alive into his presence. Having come to where Amasis was encamped, Patarbemis bade him return with him to Court; but the rebel leader, aware that his plans were known and realizing that he could expect no mercy of the King, only gave the messenger a rude answer. Patarbemis, however, who had known Amasis of old and would have helped him if he could, exhorted him to obey the King's commands and trust to his clemency.

"Thou wouldst have me put a noose about my own neck," said Amasis; "but if I must suffer, it shall not be thus tamely. Go back to thy royal master and tell him that I hasten to come into his presence, bringing others with me."

Then Patarbemis could not fail to understand his meaning, and had any doubts lingered in his mind of his friend's faithlessness, the preparations going on

The Shadow of the End

around would have dispelled them; so, turning away, he rode swiftly back to the King to tell him of these things. But when Hophra saw him coming without Amasis he fell into a terrible fury, and commanded that he should be seized and bound, and his ears and nose cut off. Then the rest of the Egyptians who had hitherto espoused the King's cause, shocked by such shameless outrage toward a noble Egyptian and a faithful servant, went over to the rebels, and put themselves and all they had at the disposal of Amasis.

Thus abandoned by his own people, Hophra quickly mustered his Greek troops, to the number of 30,000 men, and marched out from Sais against the rebel host. The two armies met near the city of Momemphis, and though the Greeks fought bravely they were worsted in the battle, overcome by the multitude of their enemies. Hophra himself fell prisoner to Amasis, and was led back a captive to the palace whence he had fared forth so proudly. The new King, however, did not treat him harshly, allowing him full freedom in his goings-out and comings-in, and showing all honour and respect to his former master. But the followers of Amasis murmured against him, saying he was wrong to show mercy to one who had been his bitter enemy and who had sought to enslave them also; wherefore he delivered Hophra into their hands to do with him as seemed good to them. And they took him out and strangled him, and buried him in the tomb of his fathers in the great temple at Sais.

So the ancient line of the Egyptian kings came to an end, and a man of the people sat upon the throne. Because he was of humble origin the Egyptians were not disposed to show him the honour and reverence due to a king; and Amasis, who was both witty and clever, determined to convict them by their own words of their inconsistency. He took a large golden bath, in which many of his guests had been wont to wash their hands and feet, and he made of it an image of one of the gods, which he then caused to be set up in a public place in the city; whereupon the Egyptians flocked thither in great numbers and worshipped the image with all reverence. Seeing this was so, Amasis assembled all the chief men of the city and thus questioned them.

"The statue that is newly set up in the city, wherefore do ye all run to worship it?" he asked.

"Because it is the semblance of our god to whom reverence is due," said the spokesman of the assembly.

"But know ye not that this image was once the bath into which ye washed off impurities from hands and feet?"

"We know it, O King," was the reply. "But, now it is changed and is an image of the god, it is meet that worship be paid to it."

"It matters not then what a thing was before," said the King; "even that which was put to the basest uses is worthy of the highest honours when its station is changed. Is it so?"

The Shadow of the End

"O King, you read our hearts," said the courtier.

"Out of your own mouths do I condemn you," said the monarch. "Lo, I, who erst was one like you am now raised to be King over you, yet I receive not the honour due to my rank. Go now, and see to it that I am treated henceforth as your King and master."

With these words he dismissed them, nor had he again to complain of lack of reverence from his subjects.

On another occasion certain of his courtiers, who disliked the way he passed his time, ventured to remonstrate with him. It was the King's custom to transact business and attend to affairs of state from sunrise until the market-hour, when the people went abroad in the streets to buy and sell; the rest of the day he spent in feasting and merrymaking, or otherwise diverting himself. These courtiers came to him and said it was not proper that the King should waste so much time in levity; he ought to sit upon the throne and occupy the whole day in attending to state matters, as had done the kings before him.

Amasis heard them to the end in silence, and then said : "When the archer hath used his bow and would lay it aside, he unstringeth it; for were it always kept taut the string would fray and the bow lose its suppleness, and fail him in time of need. So it is with men. If they are always at work and their minds fretted with carking cares, they grow moody and depressed, and lose vigour of both mind and body. For this reason I divide my time between work and pleasure."

Although the Greek troops in Egypt had fought against Amasis, he bore them no ill will for that, and even cultivated acquaintance with the lands whence they came. In this way he came to know a king named Polycrates, ruler of one of the Greek islands, and the two monarchs became fast friends. Polycrates was a man of great ability, and he quickly conquered all the neighbouring islands, making himself king over them. Wherever he went victory attended him, and his successes were so remarkable that Amasis grew alarmed. So one day he wrote his friend a letter; and this is what he said.

"Amasis to Polycrates King of Samos, Greeting! The news of thy successes hath been brought to me, and for a time I, as thy friend and ally, rejoiced thereat. But no tidings of any reverse, be it even a trifling one, having been reported, I joy no longer, for I know the gods are envious of thee. My wish for myself and for those whom I love is to be now prosperous, now unfortunate, thus preserving the balance 'twixt good and ill fortune. Never yet have I heard of anyone being always successful who did not in the end suffer some terrible calamity, and come to utter ruin. Now, therefore, give ear to my words, and meet thy unfailing good luck in this wise. Bethink thee which of thy possessions thou prizest most and art most loath to part with; then take it and cast it far from thee so that it may never come to thee again. And if thy good fortune thenceforward be not chequered with ill, keep thyself from harm by doing again as I have counselled."

When Polycrates read this letter he pondered over what his friend had written, and came to the conclusion that the advice was good; so he thought upon all the valuables he possessed, considering which it would grieve him most to lose. After long reflection he decided that his best-loved treasure was a signet-ring he was wont to wear, an emerald set in gold, of exceeding cunning workmanship. Thereupon he bade a boat be manned, in which he was rowed out into the sea, and when he was far from the land he took the ring, and, in the sight of all there, cast it into the deep. This done, he returned home and gave vent to his sorrow.

Now it came to pass some six days later that a fisherman caught amongst other fry a fish so large and beautiful that he deemed it a fit present for a king; so he took it up to the royal palace, where he happened to meet Polycrates himself. On being asked what he sought there, he knelt before the King and said, "O sire, this morning I caught a splendid fish, and though I am a poor man who live by my trade, I did not take it to market, for I said to myself, 'This fish is truly worthy of the table of the King,' and straightway I brought it here to give it to your Majesty."

Polycrates, on seeing the fish, replied, "Thou didst well, friend, to bring it hither. Nothing shalt thou lose by thy gift. Take it to the kitchen, and come and sup with me to-night."

The poor man, overjoyed at this great honour, carried the fish to the cook, and then hurried home to prepare for the coming feast.

Meanwhile the servants took the prize and began at once to clean it; but judge of their surprise when, on cutting it open, they found within its belly the very ring their master had cast into the sea. With shouts of joy they seized upon it and, hastening to Polycrates, told him how the ring had been found; but, instead of showing delight as they had expected, the King received their news in silence and with troubled mien. For in this accident he saw the hand of Fate, refusing to allow him to juggle with his lot; and forthwith he wrote a letter to Amasis of Egypt telling him all that he had done and what had come of his schemes.

Amasis was grieved on hearing what had chanced, for he believed that the gods were conspiring against his friend's happiness. He therefore wrote a second letter to Polycrates and sent it by a trusty messenger.

"Amasis to his well-beloved friend Polycrates, Greeting! The account of the ring which thou didst send to me I have read with unfeigned sorrow, for, in sooth, I see in these things the finger of Fate directed against thee. Wherefore I break off the bonds of friendship that have hitherto united us, and pray I may never hear of thee again. This I do, not because I would desert thee, but that I may escape the bitter grief which the news of the sad end in store for thee

The Shadow of the End

would cause me; for I would fain think of thee always as I do now, in the heyday of health and prosperity. Fare thee well!"

Many years afterward that which Amasis foreboded came to pass, for Polycrates, who had been beguiled into Asia by the fair promises of a Persian officer, was shamefully done to death and his body hung upon a cross.

Like the kings of Egypt before him, Amasis sought to glorify the gods by adding to the temples built in their honour. The temple of Neith at Sais was the one that received his greatest gifts, and before it he built a huge gateway with lofty towers that looked far out over the plain. To it also he gave a number of colossal statues and several sphinxes like that near Memphis, only smaller. But the most wonderful of all his works was a chamber made of a single block of stone. This stone had been quarried at Elephantine in the far south of the country, and had taken three years to convey from the quarry down the river to Sais, no less than 2000 labourers, all of whom were skilled boatmen, being engaged in the task. Its length outside was thirty-three feet, its breadth twenty-two feet, and its height twelve feet; and inside the length measured thirty feet, the breadth nineteen feet, and the height eight feet, a wondrous piece of work indeed when it is remembered that the roof formed part of the one block of stone, the chamber being hollowed out of the solid mass.

At last it arrived without mishap at the city of Sais,

and a great festival had been arranged for the day when it should be transferred from the raft on which it had floated downstream to the sanctuary in the temple. The King himself was to be present and perform the ceremony of anointing. But without the temple wall an accident happened. The block was being pushed along on rollers, when one of the levers slipped, and before the man who worked it had time to escape, the mighty mass rolled back, crushing him beneath it. So overcome was the King at the sight that he gave orders for the great stone to be left where it stood.

During the reign of Amasis Egypt was more prosperous than the country had ever been before; the river was more liberal of its flood, and the land more abundant in crops. Amasis, too, gave many useful laws to his people, among them one which bade every man appear once a year before the governor of his district and tell his means of living, failing which and to prove he got an honest livelihood, he should be put to death.

Toward the end of his life he came to variance with the King of Persia; but before that monarch invaded his land Amasis died, and was buried in the temple at Sais that he had so richly adorned.

CHAPTER XX

The Glory of Sunset

The old order changeth, yielding place to new,
And God fulfils himself in many ways.

SO has it been in all ages and in all climes; so it was in Egypt. The ancient line of kings had passed away; the Persian in his turn had come and gone; and now a stranger ruled the land. But, stranger though he were, the Macedonian who had been given to the country by the death of Alexander the Great was mindful of the old-time glory of his realm, and beneath his sway Egypt rose to a height of power and greatness among the nations such as had never been surpassed.

Yet his day, too, was rapidly drawing to its close, a day of glorious sunlight, dying away in a blaze of colour and radiance born of the eastern sky itself. A Queen sat on the throne, no weak woman she, neglected and forgotten amid the majesty that clung about the King; but a woman so captivating, so alluring, so magnificent, so imperial that even to-day the world has not ceased to wrangle about her worth. The last of a noble line, she eclipsed all her ancestors in magnificence

234   Egyptian Gods and Heroes

and splendour as easily as the kings of Egypt outshone the rulers of all other climes.

Such was Cleopatra, Queen of Egypt. Early she gave proof of an iron will, no less than of the extravagant tastes for which she became famous. Her father died when she was still young, and, as was customary in Egypt, she was associated with her brother in the government of the country. But her temper could brook no opposition, and the two soon quarrelled, whereon Cleopatra with her supporters fled into Syria.

At this time Rome was mistress of the world, and claimed the overlordship of this land. So when Julius Cæsar set out for Parthia to extend the Roman Empire in the East, he resolved to put in at Alexandria and restore order in the riven country.

Well did Cleopatra know that if Cæsar were left with her brother she would have little chance of coming into her own again, and she resolved to plead her own cause with the Roman. But it was no easy matter to come to him, for he would not see her privately, which was what she sought. Howbeit Cleopatra, ready with a thousand wiles where her desires were in question, called her steward and, having wrapped herself close in the coverlet of her bed, bade him carry her by night to Cæsar's banqueting-hall. The porter, seeing only a man with a bundle, admitted him, unsuspecting; and in a trice Cleopatra stood before the famous general. He, laughing heartily at the trick she had played him, put her at her ease, asking her to sit beside him to tell

The Glory of Sunset 235

her story—and her victory was won. In her rich voice, low and infinitely sweet, a voice that bewitched every man that heard it as surely as ever Siren did the wearied sailor, she pleaded with him until dawn. But long before Aurora, blushing rosy red, came forth, mighty Cæsar was undone, ready and eager to grant all that she might ask.

It was not to be expected that the King of Egypt, Ptolemy XII, would submit to Cæsar's biased judgments without a struggle, and for nine months the Roman troops were engaged in quelling the rebels. Finally their power was utterly shattered in a fierce battle, the King himself being numbered with the slain.

In the name of Rome Cæsar now gave Egypt to Cleopatra, and betrothed her to the heir to the throne, brother to the dead King; but, as Cæsar's friend, the Queen it was who really held the reins of power. Together these two made a royal progress up the Nile as far as Ethiopia, travelling in a gilded barge and escorted by four hundred ships with all the officers and nobles of the realm aboard. Then Cæsar was recalled to Rome, and, loath to part with so fair an enchantress, he invited Cleopatra to go with him. To Rome she went, there staying until Cæsar's death, whereon she returned to Egypt.

Not many months elapsed before new troubles arose. Cleopatra could not suffer another to wield the sceptre with her, and strife and confusion prevailed. Hence when Antony, friend to the dead Cæsar, arrived in Cilicia, having been sent by Rome to wage war against her enemies in Asia, he summoned Cleopatra to come before him to answer for her stewardship. Once, and twice, and thrice he sent, and one and all his messages received scant attention; then when at last she came, she came not as a suppliant praying Rome's forgiveness, but as a stately Queen.

In a beautiful white boat, with gilded stern and sails of royal purple, its oars of solid silver beating time to the tune of flute and pipe and lute, Cleopatra sailed up the river Cydnus to the spot where Antony was encamped. She reclined beneath a canopy of cloth of gold, and boys on either side fanned her with waving plumes of ostrich feathers set in gold, while the most comely of her maidens, dressed as nymphs and nereids, lined the bulwarks. Choice flowers of richest fragrance strewed the decks, and golden censers wafted spicy odours across the waters to the crowds that lined the banks. The news of her arrival was brought to Antony, who sent for her to join him at the evening repast; but she replied it behoved him rather to come to her, so, wishing to be courteous, he went.

He found the preparations made for him magnificent beyond compare. Costly viands and delicate were there in plenty, and choicest wines ran free; gentle music lulled the senses as he ate, while dusky maids flitted to and fro before him. But nothing pleased

The Glory of Sunset 237

him so much as the arrangement of the lights and their number; for on a sudden there were lowered upon them many branches of trees, with twinkling lights disposed ingeniously amid the leaves, in squares and circles and other devices, in such profusion that the eye was dazzled and the brain bewildered.

And thus did Antony in his turn fall victim to the charms of the Egyptian Queen. In dulcet tones she laid her case before him, and the Roman general was her slave. Instead of carrying on the war against Parthia he sailed away with Cleopatra to Alexandria, and there began a round of revelry and delights such as the world has seldom seen.

Fearing lest her lover should grow sated with his pleasures, Cleopatra never for a moment left him; by day she hunted or fished with him, and by night they diced over their wine. She even joined him on those wild escapades when he wandered through the city, joking and drinking with the common folk. Both were dressed in servant's guise, yet few there were who knew them not. But she was ready to make fun even at his expense, when she knew that he was safely in her toils.

Cleopatra was fond of angling, and one day she arranged an entertainment on her royal barge, at which her guests should compete with each other in catching fish. Antony had cast his line for some time to no purpose, and the Queen, whose growing catch lay shining in the sun beside her, rallied him on his want of success.

"Clearly thy art is not one of peace," she said, "for thou failest here where my women succeed."

Antony frowned, for the taunt liked him not; and he secretly bade his sailors go down and hook on his line some of the fish that had been caught. He then started to haul them in so rapidly as to excite amaze in all around.

"My luck hath turned," he said. "Even the fair Cleopatra could scarce do better than this." And on the word he pulled in another fish.

"In sooth, luck always attendeth thee, soon or late," said she, smiling. "Is there aught in which my Antony could fail?"

The Roman smiled back, pleased with the flattery, not seeing the twinkle that lurked in her eye.

Next day another fishing-match was held, and, beforehand, Cleopatra called her best diver to her and gave him a secret order. Barely had the gay company cast their lines when Antony felt a pull on his, and, dragging it in with some difficulty, landed a large fish upon the deck. But, instead of hailing it with cries of admiration, the merry throng burst into peals of laughter, for the fish he had caught was one found only in the Euxine Sea, *and it was salted.*

Antony was furious at the trick that had been played him, but Cleopatra, going to him, quickly calmed his wrath. "Leave angling and the gentle arts to the peaceful Egyptians," she said, "and do thou seek honour in arms, where my beloved Antony hath no peer."

The Glory of Sunset

When Antony left Rome he was at odds with the emperor Octavianus Cæsar, and he now learned that his wife Fulvia had been obliged to flee the country. Roused at length to a sense of duty he left Egypt to meet her, but as he set sail news came that she was dead, so he directed his ships straight toward Italy. The quarrel with Octavianus was composed, and Antony married Cæsar's sister Octavia, a good and noble woman, beautiful as good; whence it was augured that the strife which had torn Rome in twain would now be healed.

Meanwhile the Parthians had invaded Syria, and again Antony marched forth to subdue them. After a long campaign and much loss of life he forced them into submission, and thereupon returned to a place on the Syrian coast called the "White Village," whence he sent to Egypt for Cleopatra to come and join him. Soon after her arrival news came that his wife Octavia was on her way to meet him, with men and stores and money.

When Cleopatra heard of this she feared lest the advent of Octavia would bring her influence over Antony to an end, and she sought to entice him away before his wife arrived. She ate sparingly and seemed as though she were ill, and took care that Antony should oft-times find her in tears, which, however, on his coming she quickly wiped away, as though not wishing that he should see her thus. Her friends, too, reproached him for his hardness of heart, saying that she was wasting away for love of him, and that, unless he took pity on her, she would surely die. He was in sore need of the supplies his wife was bringing; but at last, overcome by his love of her, he hearkened to their pleadings, and returned with Cleopatra to Alexandria.

The career of feasting and enjoyment now began anew, and nightly entertainments were given, when Cleopatra would attire herself as the goddess Isis, while Antony represented Osiris and her children lesser gods. During the day hunting expeditions and excursions up the river Nile were arranged to beguile the hours. Thus with all her powers did Cleopatra seek to hold her lover fascinated; while he, on his part, let slip no occasion whereby he might make manifest his devotion to her.

Once at a banquet given by Antony he caused to be set up on a lofty dais two golden thrones, one for the Queen and one for him, the while her children were provided with other thrones below them. Calling upon the assembled guests to mark his words, Antony spake.

"In the name of Imperial Rome, I, as her sole envoy in the East, do here command you to pay homage and fealty to Cleopatra for the kingdoms of Egypt, Libya, Cyprus, and Lower Syria, over which she doth rule henceforth as Queen, having with her in the government thereof only her son Cæsarion; and because of her greatness and might she shall be styled hereafter Queen of Kings. And to her son Alexander we give the provinces of Armenia, Media, and Parthia, to have and

The Glory of Sunset 241

to hold in the name of Rome; and to her son Ptolemy the kingdoms of Phœnicia, Syria, and Cilicia; and they two shall each be styled King of Kings. See ye that due homage be paid to them as to us."

Thus in a breath did Antony part with all the hard-won conquests of Rome in the East.

In the meantime Octavia had returned to Rome, and her brother Octavianus Cæsar, furious at the insult Antony had put upon her, brought the matter before the Senate, and spoke in such terms of him and Cleopatra that the council hearkened to his wishes and declared war on Egypt. Antony accepted the challenge, and set sail with 800 ships for the isle of Samos in the Ionian Sea, whither he bade his friends and vassals repair. At first he would have left Cleopatra behind, but she entreated him so pitifully not to go without her that he consented and they sailed together.

For many days they stopped in Samos, where feasts and entertainments were given by the many petty kings who, in response to Antony's command, had forgathered there. Stirred at length by tidings of Cæsar's approach, Antony made preparations for the coming battle. But, against the advice of all his captains, he resolved to fight on sea and not on land; for Cleopatra had brought sixty ships of war and 200,000 talents of money to his aid, and wished that battle should be offered to the foe on sea—and with Antony her will prevailed over all.

The fight took place near Actium, and, although

Antony was outmatched by Cæsar's fleet, he might yet have saved the day but for the cowardice of Cleopatra. She, thinking all hope was gone, gave command that her ships, which had been idly waiting apart, should hoist sail and make for Egypt; and Antony, at sight of her desertion, basely forgetting duty and honour for the love of his enchantress, leapt into a boat and was rowed alongside her ship. The Queen, perceiving who it was, had him brought aboard, and together they sailed away from the fight; and the rest of the fleet, abandoned by their commander in direst hour of need, were compelled to yield.

The bulk of Antony's army, numbering nineteen legions of foot and 12,000 horse, were still on shore, and refused to believe the report of his flight. Such confidence had they in their old commander, and so faithful were they to the leader they admired and loved, that for seven long, anxious days they turned deaf ears to every message from Octavian, firmly believing that Antony would reappear to take charge of them and lead them on to victory. But when at last their officers began to steal away, at first by ones and twos, and then by tens and scores, they knew that all was lost, and in broken-hearted silence sent in their submission.

The fugitives touched at Prætorium in Libya, and thence Antony sent Cleopatra on to Egypt. After she had gone he became a prey to shame and sorrow, and, calling his few faithful followers around him, he bade them leave him.

The Glory of Sunset

"Why stay with me?" he said. "My day is spent. Mark Antony, who had the world at his feet, is brought to naught. Yet have I a few friends in Rome who will treat you well, and for whom I here give you letters asking them to help you for my sake. Go ye down to the harbour and take my ship. 'Tis full of treasure. Divide that among you, and sail quickly to Rome while yet there is time. Why stand ye there?" he cried, as they moved not. "Will ye die with me?" and he drew his sword as if to slay himself. But his friends, perceiving that he was distraught with grief, prevented him, and sent him on to Alexandria.

When he came there he found Cleopatra engaged in a daring project of escape. This was no less than to convey her ships across the narrow neck of sand between the Mediterranean and the Red Sea, and so to pass into the lands beyond Arabia, hoping thereafter to be able to live in peace, far from war and slavery. But the first ships carried over being burnt by the Arabs, she abandoned the idea, and gave orders that all the approaches into Egypt should be fortified against the coming of Cæsar, knowing full well that her defeat and capture would lead to her appearing in his triumphal procession at Rome, a shame and humiliation to which her proud spirit could never submit.

Antony, on reaching Alexandria, would no longer dwell with Cleopatra in the palace, building instead a house on a rock near the isle called Pharos, where he lived alone, sunk in despair. Then, strange to tell, as news poured in that first one and then another of his sometime allies were going over to the enemy, his spirits rose, and, when he had naught left to him but Egypt, he again joined the Queen. These two now instituted an order called the Order of Those Who Would Die Together, to which were admitted only those who swore a solemn oath to stand by the Queen even to death, let what might betide. The noblest and the wealthiest of the city flocked to give in their names, and an era of gorgeous extravagance opened surpassing all that had gone before.

Meantime Cæsar was advancing on Egypt, and, when he drew nigh, Antony sent letters to him, asking that Egypt should be given to Cleopatra and her children; for himself he sought nothing save only to be allowed to live in Egypt as a private citizen, or, were that too much to be granted, to retire to Athens. Neither had any hope that Octavian would hearken to their plea; and Cleopatra, who was resolved to die rather than to fall into his hands, had brought to her all manner of poisonous drugs, whose virtues she assayed on the criminals in the prisons under sentence of death. But, not satisfied with these, she next brought many venomous creatures and set them to fight each other, that she might note the effects of their poison. In this way she found that the bite of the asp, that sacred serpent whose symbol was the brightest ornament in the Egyptian diadem, was the quickest and least painful

The Glory of Sunset 245

in its action, causing its victim to fall into a deep sleep from which it waked no more.

When Cæsar's reply came, Cleopatra was offered all honourable treatment would she put Antony to death or drive him forth from the country. "Hearest thou, beloved?" said Antony, as he read the letter. "Which fate dost thou choose for me?"

"The fool!" cried Cleopatra in a fury. "Thinketh he I should buy safety at the price of thy life? Go, my Antony, make ready our defences, and show this upstart how we receive his offer."

So well did the Roman drill the Egyptian troops that, when Cæsar came, Antony defeated him in open battle. This notwithstanding, several of his officers deserted to the force of Rome, and Antony resolved to crush his enemy on sea. He stood on a little knoll to watch the issue of the fray, and, as his ships drew near the enemy's, he waited impatiently for the attack. What was his surprise to see them making friendly signals to the Roman vessels, and, on their coming together, sail away with them into the harbour. At the same time one came running to say that his horse-soldiers had gone over to Cæsar; and, thinking he had been betrayed by Cleopatra, he rushed back into the city, crying aloud against her.

"Is it for this, then, that I have loved thee, Cleopatra!" he cried. "Name and fame, riches and honour, power and glory, yea, home and country, all have I given up for thee, and now thou too dost leave me. Unhappy man that I am!" Just then a messenger came in to him saying that Cleopatra was dead, having been unable to brook defeat and Antony's wrath. He believing it exclaimed, "Now, Antony, why delay longer? Fate hath taken away the only pretext for which thou couldst wish to live." Taking off his armour, "I grieve not that thou art dead, my Queen," he said, "for I shall soon be with thee; but it distresseth me sore that so great a general should be of tardier courage than a woman."

So he called his servant Eros, whom he bade take his sword and slay him. And Eros, the tears coursing down his cheeks in bitter sorrow for the master who always had been kind to him, drew the sword and made as though to carry our Antony's wish; but, turning suddenly, he passed the blade through his own body. "'Tis bravely done, Eros," said Antony. "Thou showest thy master how to do what he feared to do himself." And, picking up the sword, he stabbed himself.

The wound, however, was not at once mortal, and he called on his friends around to take the weapon and put him out of pain; but they in affright fled from the room, and Antony was left alone until Diomede, Cleopatra's secretary, came to say that she would speak with him.

Now the Queen on hearing that Antony was frenzied at the faithlessness of his men and, as he thought, of her, had shut herself up in a lofty tower which she had

The Glory of Sunset

aforetime built as her tomb, and in which she had gathered all her treasures of gold and silver, emeralds, sapphires, and pearls, and many precious and quaint carvings, with much touchwood on top of all, intending to set fire to it should Octavianus gain the city. But now she sent for her lover; and he, as soon as he knew she was not dead, bade them carry him to her. On reaching the tower Cleopatra would not suffer the door to be opened, but lowered a rope from an upper window, by which she and her two waiting-women drew him up.

"Oh, my beloved Antony," she cried, as she saw the wound in his body; "hath it then come to this? Woe, woe is me that I should live to see my lord thus brought low!" Amid bitter tears and lamentations she strove to staunch the flow of blood, but her efforts were of no avail. She beat her hands on face and breast, tearing the delicate flesh with her nails in the frenzy of her grief. But Antony smiling said, "Weep not, loved one. I have lived my day. But thou art young. Make thy peace with Cæsar, and thou mayest yet live long to rule Egypt." Then, calling for wine, he drank eagerly, for the thirst from his wound was great, and shortly after, murmuring words of love to the Queen who had ruined his life, he fell back and died.

When Cæsar learned that Antony was dead he retired to his tent and wept bitterly, as at the loss of a dear friend; for, albeit they had been at war with each other, they were both Romans, and had once been friends and brothers.

Many kings and princes came to the emperor to sue for Antony's body, that they might give it honourable burial; but he refused them all, saying that Cleopatra had first right, and offering her safe conduct during the funeral. So she prepared a magnificent tomb, in which was a sarcophagus of red granite with divers sculptures carved upon it; and there, with solemn pomp and dignity, she laid her lord to rest.

The bitterness of her grief, and the wounds she had inflicted in her breast as she wildly beat upon it, brought on a high fever, and for many days she lay nigh unto death. In truth she wished it might so fall out; but Cæsar, suspecting she was trying thus to end her life, threatened such dire punishments for her children should she die that she strove to get well. One day the emperor visited her, and after a long talk she seemed disposed to go to Rome, whither she learned he was about to depart by way of Syria. It may be that she hoped to beguile his heart while they journeyed, as she had oft-times done with others; mayhap she was too sorely grieved at heart to heed what further evil might befall. Howbeit, on finding that she would be sent to Rome before him, she requested liberty to pray and offer sacrifice at Antony's tomb, and this being granted her, she was borne in a litter to the place where he was buried.

For long she gazed at the granite coffin which held

The Glory of Sunset   249

all that was once a mighty Roman, the tears streaming down her cheeks the while; and as she looked, with eyes that seemed to pierce the stone, she knew at last how dear this man had been to her. From childhood's days she had been wont to have court paid to her. The beautiful face, crowned with a wreath of red-gold hair, the graceful figure and sinuous form; above all, the sweet, low voice that held enthralled all who heard it, even as the nightingale on summer eve holds the listener spellbound, had brought her unbounded homage from every man she met. Such homage she had taken as her right, recking not of the lives that had been cast away by reason of it. And not till now, not till this supreme moment when she must bid farewell to all that she had loved, to go and die a captive in far-distant Rome, did she know how infinitely more dear to her had Antony been than all the rest.

"O dearest Antony," she sobbed, "not long since these hands came here to bury thee. Then were they free; now they are captive, and I am watched by servile guards lest I harm my body and so deprive their master of the glory of his triumph. Whilst thou lived, my beloved, nothing could divide us; now death doth threaten to put us far asunder, for they would carry me captive to Rome, there to die in shame. But no, it shall not be. In life were we ever together; in death shall we be undivided. Thou art gone, my loved one, but not for long shall thy Cleopatra wait. Soon shall death release her from the bonds of shame and sorrow, and beyond the shadows shall she join thee again. Farewell, my lord, 'tis but for a little while."

As she spoke her voice died away until it was but a whisper, soft as the breeze that stirs the fen-grown sedge. Her tears ceased, and now, her face drawn by pain and grief yet full of quiet purpose, she rose, and strewed rich-scented flowers on his tomb. Bending over it she passionately kissed the cold stone, and then was borne back to her tower.

That night she took a sumptuous meal, for Cæsar's spies were about her watching all she did, and she sought to deceive them. As she finished a country fellow brought in a basket of figs, and Cleopatra, after praising their size and richness, accepted them and rewarded the man. Next she took from her dress a letter which she had written and sealed, and sent it by the guards to Cæsar; which done, she put every one out of the tower except her two tiring-maids.

Alone, she turned back the leaves from the basket of figs; and there, coiled beneath them, its beady eyes glittering in the torchlight, lay a deadly asp. Taking it in her hand she said, "Pretty creature, shunned of all others, how welcome thou art to me! Thy bite I fear not, nay I seek it, for it bringeth peace and rest. And in that peace I shall meet my Antony again."

At the thought a smile came to the grief-lined face; and, picking up a golden spindle, she pricked the serpent, which in its anger sprang forward and bit her arm. Dropping the asp she whispered, "I come, dear Antony, my lord, my husband, I come;" and, rising from the chair, she staggered to her bed. When Cæsar arrived—for on reading the letter and finding only prayers and entreaties that she might be buried with Antony he guessed what she was minded to do—he broke into the tower, but he was too late. There, on a bed of gold, set out in all her royal robes and jewels, lay Cleopatra, dead.

Thus was Cæsar balked of the crowning glory of his triumph; but, though sorely disappointed, he honoured her brave spirit, and gave orders that she should be buried in Antony's tomb with imperial honours. So in the tomb she had built for her lover side by side they lay, these twain; the honoured general of a modern Rome, who by millions of her subjects had been hailed as lord and emperor, and of ancient Egypt the most brilliant and the most renowned of all her queens: two of princely mould who might have ruled the world, yet counted all as naught for sake of love.

CHAPTER XXI

Light upon the Darkness

THUS passed away the once mighty empire of Egypt—the great, the glorious, the supreme. The power that had been hers had gone to another, the honour and homage she had received from all the world were hers no more. Her temples, whose hallowed aisles had echoed to the march of priests and chant of white-robed maidens, became the homes of owls and bats; her palaces, where kings had lived in gorgeous splendour surrounded by ten thousand guards, were levelled to the ground; her cities, whose size and grandeur had aroused the envy of the world, were buried under the ever-shifting sand so that their place was unknown of men; even her tongue was forgotten, and her story, carved with such infinite patience by her scribes in hardest stone, was understood of none: nay, the strange devices that met men's eyes on towering obelisk and ruined temple helped but to deepen the mystery of this mystic and enchanted land.

This change had not been suddenly wrought by the death of Cleopatra. Long before her day the knell of Egypt had been rung. With the Persian conquerors began her final downfall, and, though Alexander might stave off the evil day, it could not be long after his death ere the blow fell. When the Roman came her strength had already been sapped away, and she was the easy prey of any hand strong enough to hold the sceptre.

So Egypt became the vassal of imperial Rome, and for long centuries men knew little of the greatness and glory that had been hers in ages gone. Tales there were in plenty, tales of mighty warriors fighting against fierce enemies who fell like corn before the scythe in face of the invincible arm of Egypt, tales of sovereign kings at whose nod a countless host would rise to go forth and do battle with the foe. Were not the vast temple ruins, the lofty columns, the massive pyramids proof of a people that had been greater to conceive and execute than any other the world has seen? But of this people, their work, their lives, their faith and beliefs, little could be gleaned, for with the passing of their empire had gone those who alone could read the tale aright. A few there were remaining of the priestly class who knew something of the writing, but with the newer times and newer faiths their interest in it waned, and ere long all knowledge of these pictures and their meaning was buried in the tomb.

So the long years passed away, and the desert sands kept safe their secret. And it came to pass that about

254   Egyptian Gods and Heroes

a hundred years ago Fate gave to man that which the studious had waited for. The Rosetta Stone, the large slab of black stone of which mention has been made, on which was engraved a royal decree in hieroglyphic and demotic and Greek characters, was the clue to the mysteries that they had searched for, the key to a fairyland of wonders such as even the most fanciful had never dreamed of. By a comparison of the various tongues upon it, and then with inscriptions on other monuments, an Egyptian alphabet was made out; and little by little, as the various ruins and buried treasures have been unearthed, their story has been pieced together.

Something of what has been revealed to us you have here read. But most of these tales belong to the day when even Egypt, old as she is, was still young, and to the time when her kings held sway over almost all that was not lost in barbarism. Of that which brought her from her high estate little has been said. Yet it is easy to see what led to her ruin. Whenever men put self-interest before the common weal, when they give up self-discipline to live in luxurious ease, when they forget their ancient faiths that have sustained them in the hour of trial and stress, and scoff at honour and virtue, the end is not far off. And thus it was in Egypt. Before the days of Amasis the canker had taken root. The magnificence of Cleopatra was but an echo of the ancient glory, that with her passed away into silence;

nay, in truth, it was founded on those very evils that destroyed her country.

So if you are tempted to imagine that we to-day are greatly superior to the people who lived in Egypt in those far-off times, and to pity them because you think they knew so little, ponder for a moment on the words of that sage who, nearly 6000 years ago, spoke thus to his son. " Be not proud because thou art learned, but discourse with the ignorant man as with the wise. For no limit can be set to skill, neither is there any craftsman that possesseth full knowledge. ... If thou be among people, make to thyself love, the beginning and the end of life. ... If thou be a man of position, be gracious when thou hearkenest to the words of a suppliant. If thou desire that thine actions be good, keep thyself from all malice, and beware of covetousness, which is a grievous ill: it gathereth unto itself all evils, it is the girdle of all wickedness. But the man that is just flourisheth, truth goeth in his footsteps and therein he hath his abiding-place."

And there is surely not much more to learn if from your heart you can say what every Egyptian believed he must say, when brought face to face with Osiris in the Hall of Judgment, while his heart swung slowly in the balance against the symbol of eternal Truth. " I have spoken no lies; I have brought sorrow to none; I have not dealt deceitfully nor acted with guile; I have not stirred up strife. I have not spoken ill of any man, nor have I stopped my ears against right and truth. I have given bread to the hungry and water unto them that thirst, clothing unto the naked and a boat to the shipwrecked mariner. I have done that which is right and pure; and my God have I faithfully served in spirit and in truth."

Additional Egyptian Legends

THE COMING OF THE GREAT QUEEN

Ancient Egyptian Legends, M A Murray
1913

Now Amon-Ra, king of the gods, sat upon his throne, and around him stood the greatest of the gods and goddesses. On his right was Osiris crowned with the great White Crown of the South Land; on his left was Mentu, god of war, and on the head of Mentu were two great feathers and the flashing disk of the sun. With Osiris were the twin goddesses Isis and Nephthys, beside them stood Hathor, goddess of love, whom the Greeks call Aphrodite; Horus, the son of Isis, with the far-seeing eyes of the hawk; and Anubis, son of Nephthys, the faithful guardian of Isis. With Mentu were Atmu, the god of the sunset; Shu and his twin-sister Tefnut; Geb the earth-god, and Nut the sky-goddess. These two are the oldest of the gods, from whom all others proceed.

Amon-Ra, king of the gods, sat upon his throne and looked upon the land of Egypt, and he spoke, saying, "I will create a queen to rule over Tamery, I will unite the Two Lands in peace for her,

THE COMING OF THE GREAT QUEEN

and in her hands I will place the whole world. Egypt and Syria, Nubia and Punt, the land of the Gods, shall be under her sway." And when he had spoken there was silence among the gods.

While he yet spoke, Thoth entered into his presence, Thoth, the twice-great, the maker of magic, the lord of Khemennu. He listened to the words of Amon-Ra, king of the gods, and in the silence that followed he spoke:

"O Amon-Ra, Lord of the thrones of the Two Lands, King of the gods, Maker of men. Behold in the Black Land in the palace of the king is a maiden, fair and beautiful is she in all her limbs. Aahmes is her name, and she is wife to the king of Egypt. She alone can be the mother of the great Queen, whom thou wilt create to rule over the Two Lands. She is in the palace of the king. Come, let us go to her."

Now the form of Thoth is the form of an ibis, that he may fly swiftly through the air and none may know him, and as an ibis he went to the palace of the king. But Amon-Ra took upon himself the shape of the king of Egypt. Great was the majesty of Amon-Ra, splendid his adornments. On his neck was the glittering collar of gold and precious stones, on his arms were bracelets of pure gold and electrum, and on his head were two plumes; by the plumes alone could men know the King of the gods. In one hand he carried

THE COMING OF THE GREAT QUEEN

the sceptre of power, in the other the emblem of life. Glorious was he as the sun at midday, and the perfumes of the land of Punt were around him.

In the palace of the king of Egypt was queen Aahmes, and it was night. She lay upon her couch, and sleep was upon her eyelids. Like a jewel was she in her beauty, and the chamber in which she slept was like the setting of the jewel; black bronze and electrum, acacia wood and ebony, were the adornments of the palace, and her couch was in the form of a fierce lion.

Through the two Great Doors of the palace went the gods; none saw them, none beheld them. And with them came Neith, goddess of Sais, and Selk the scorpion goddess. On the head of Neith were the shield and crossed arrows; on the head of Selk a scorpion bearing in each claw the emblem of life.

The fragrance of the perfumes of Punt filled the chamber, and queen Aahmes awoke and beheld Amon-Ra, King of the gods, Maker of men. In majesty and beauty he appeared before her, and her heart was filled with joy. He held towards her the sign of life, and in her hand he laid the sign of life and the sceptre of power. And Neith and Selk lifted the couch on which the queen reposed and held it high in the air, that she might be raised above the ground, on which mortal men live, while she spoke with the immortal Gods.

THE COMING OF THE GREAT QUEEN

Then Amon-Ra returned and was enthroned among the Gods. And he summoned to his presence Khnum the creator, he who fashions the bodies of men, who dwells beside the rushing waters of the cataract. To Khnum he gave command saying, "O Khnum, fashioner of the bodies of men, fashion for me my daughter, she who shall be the great Queen of Egypt. For I will give to her all life and satisfaction, all stability and all joy of heart for ever."

Khnum the creator, the fashioner of the bodies of men, the dweller by the cataract, made answer to Amon-Ra, "I will form for thee thy daughter, and her form shall be more glorious than the Gods, for the greatness of her dignity as King of the South and North."

Then he brought his potter's wheel, and took clay, and with his hands he fashioned the body of the daughter of queen Aahmes and the body of her *ka*. And the body of the child and the body of the *ka* were alike in their limbs and their faces, and none but the Gods could know them apart. Beautiful were they with the beauty of Amon-Ra, more glorious were they than the Gods.

Beside the potter's wheel knelt Hekt, lady of Herur, goddess of birth. In each hand she held the sign of life, and as the wheel turned and the bodies were fashioned, she held it towards them that life might enter into the lifeless clay.

Then Khnum, the fashioner of the bodies of

THE COMING OF THE GREAT QUEEN

men, and Hekt the goddess of birth, came to the palace of the king of Egypt; and with them came Isis, the great Mother, and her sister Nephthys; Meskhent also and Ta-urt, and Bes the protector of children. The spirits of Pé and the spirits of Dep came with them to greet the daughter of Amon-Ra and of queen Aahmes.

And when the child appeared, the goddesses rejoiced, and the spirits of Pé and the spirits of Dep chanted praises to her honour, for the daughter of Amon-Ra was to sit upon the throne of Horus of the Living, and rule the Land of Egypt to the glory of the Gods. Hatshepsut was she called, Chief of Noble Women, divine of Diadems, favourite of the Goddesses, beloved of Amon-Ra. And to her the Gods granted that she should be mistress of all lands within the circuit of the sun, and that she should appear as king upon the throne of Horus before the glories of the Great House. And upon her was the favour of Amon-Ra for ever.

www.ingramcontent.com/pod-product-compliance
Lightning Source LLC
Chambersburg PA
CBHW020225170426
43201CB00007B/323